The Children's Life of Christ

ENID BLYTON

The Children's Life of Christ

Illustrated by Eileen Soper

A DRAGON BOOK

GRANADA
London Toronto Sydney New York

Published by Granada Publishing Limited in 1970
Reprinted 1973, 1975, 1983

ISBN 0 583 30149 5

First published by Methuen & Co Ltd 1943

Granada Publishing Limited
Frogmore, St Albans, Herts AL2 2NF
and
36 Golden Square, London W1R 4AH
515 Madison Avenue, New York, NY 10022, USA
117 York Street, Sydney, NSW 2000, Australia
60 International Blvd, Rexdale, Ontario R9W 6J2, Canada
61 Beach Road, Auckland, New Zealand

Printed and bound in Great Britain by
Cox & Wyman Ltd, Reading
Set in Monotype Times

FOREWORD

The life of Christ is a wonderful story to tell. It is not only full of beauty, but full of interest and drama, an ideal story to tell to children.

In a book as short as this I was faced with the alternatives of putting in everything, which would mean a kind of skimming over the surface, or of choosing out my material and dealing with it lovingly to try and bring out the inner meaning of much of the matter. I chose the second course, because children love detail in a story of this kind, and because a little, well-told, is worth a great deal of closely-packed matter which, after a time, becomes quite indigestible to children.

This explains why some of the parables and miracles are missing. I have chosen most of the important ones, especially those that children can well understand and appreciate.

I have also kept as closely as I can to the Gospel stories, because it is from these that our children are taught at school and at home, and, where possible, I have used the simple and beautiful words of the original text. I have also kept my own text and style as simple as possible, because I would like the book to appeal to children as young as four, who have to be read to, as well as to children in their 'teens. From my own experience I know that if the language is right, a story will appeal to children of any age, particularly if it holds the intense beauty and interest of a tale such as this.

I felt it to be a great honour to be asked to write this book. In all my books, whether of school-life, adventure stories, circus tales, animal or fairy tales, the underlying insistence on love, kindness, charity and justice has always been there; and now to write the life-story of the One Whose whole life and teaching exemplified these things has been a great experience and delight. I realize humbly that in many ways the book fails to be as good as I would have liked it to be, but if it succeeds in presenting to the children a clear, simple and enthralling picture of the world's most amazing and wonderful character, then I shall know that the book may perhaps be likened to a "seed that fell on good ground". And that will be the greatest reward I could have.

ENID BLYTON

January 1, 1943

CONTENTS

		Page
	Foreword	5
1	The Little Girl of Nazareth	9
2	Mary and the Angel	10
3	The Journey to Bethlehem	14
4	The Baby Jesus	17
5	The Shepherds on the Hill	18
6	The Three Wise Men	24
7	A Sad Day for Bethlehem	30
8	How Jesus Escaped	31
9	The Little Nazarene	34
10	Twelve Years Old	37
11	Jesus is Lost	41
12	Jesus Grows Up	44
13	John, the Cousin of Jesus	45
14	Jesus and Satan, the Prince of Evil	47
15	The First Friends of Jesus	49
16	Jesus Begins his Work	51
17	The Nobleman's Son	53
18	The Man by the Pool	55
19	The Man who was a Leper	59
20	The Man who Came through the Roof	61
21	The Soldier and his Servant	65
22	Jesus Meets a Funeral	67
23	The Wonderful Storyteller	69
24	The Tale of the Sower	70
25	The Tale of the Mustard Seed	72
26	The Tale of the Fisherman	72
27	The Tale of the Shepherd and the Lost Sheep	72
28	The Story of the Boy who Went Away	73

		Page
29	Jesus and the Storm	76
30	Jesus and the Madman	77
31	The Little Daughter of Jairus	80
32	The Boy with the Loaves and the Little Fishes	85
33	On the Way to Jerusalem	90
34	The Tale of the Good Samaritan	92
35	Jesus and the Little Tax-Collector	96
36	Happiness for a Blind Man	99
37	Jesus and the Children	100
38	The Rich Young Man	101
39	Jesus Enters Jerusalem	103
40	Jesus Goes to the Temple	106
41	The Widow's Gift	108
42	Jesus Warns the People	109
43	The Story of the Ten Bridesmaids	110
44	The Last Story that Jesus Told	112
45	Judas, the Traitor	113
46	The Time Draws Near	115
47	The Last Supper	116
48	In the Garden of Gethsemane	120
49	Jesus is Captured	121
50	Before the Cock Crew Twice	122
51	The Trial of Jesus	124
52	Jesus Goes before Pilate, the Roman Governor	125
53	Jesus is Punished	129
54	What Happened to the Traitor	131
55	Jesus is Crucified	132
56	Jesus Comes Again	136
57	Jesus Comes to His Disciples	139
58	Jesus Goes to Galilee	141
59	The End of the Story	143

1: THE LITTLE GIRL OF NAZARETH

Long, long ago in the little village of Nazareth there lived a small girl called Mary. The people there knew her well and loved her, because she was always ready to listen to those in trouble, and to help them.

She lived with her father and mother, and played with the other children round about. She was a dreamy, thoughtful child, who sometimes liked to be alone and think of all the things she saw and heard.

Sometimes Mary heard her mother and father talking sadly together about great days that were gone. "We are no longer a great people," said her father. "Another nation rules us."

"Who rules us?" asked Mary.

"The Romans," said her father. "They came here with their great armies, Mary. They marched along our roads. They took our country, and said that no longer should it belong to us, but to Rome!"

"The boys and girls say that Rome has conquered all the world," said Mary. "Can nobody save us and make us a great people again?"

"Yes – there is someone who will save us and be our greatest King," said her mother. "But I don't know who that will be."

"Oh, Mother – how do you know that we shall have a great saviour?" asked the little girl.

"Because God has promised us," said her mother. "And what God promises always comes to pass. I will read to you what some of our great men of old said about this wonderful King."

And then the little girl heard that some day God would send to Israel, the country in which Mary lived, a king even greater than David, the greatest king they had ever had. He should be greater than any other king on earth.

"Mother, I wish he would come soon," said Mary. "Then I should see him. Do you think he is born yet?"

Her mother sighed. "Who knows?" she said. "These are hard days for us. Surely the time is near at hand for God's promise to be fulfilled, and for our king to be sent to save us."

"It's strange to think that all great kings are tiny babies first," said Mary. "I suppose he will be born in some fine palace, and will have the most beautiful cradle, and clothes as soft as the petals of a flower. And a great princess will be his mother."

Her mother looked round the little house set in the hills where she and her family lived. "We are poor now," she said, "but you know, Mary, once upon a time our family belonged to the royal family of David."

"Then was King David my great-great-great-many-greats, great-grandfather?" asked Mary, in surprise.

Her mother nodded. "Yes. But that was long, long ago. You know Joseph, the carpenter in the village? Well, his family once belonged to the house of David, too. He will tell you about it if you ask him."

Mary thought a great deal about the king that God had promised to his people. She wished he would come soon. "If only I could see him," she thought. "If I were a royal princess I might even be his mother, and that would be wonderful. Then I could love him and help him. I will ask Joseph if he has heard of him too."

Joseph was a carpenter who lived not far from Mary's family, in the same village. He knew Mary very well and was fond of her. He talked to her whenever she came by. He too knew about the king that had been promised.

"He will come one day!" he said to Mary, as he worked at his bench. "God has promised it. Surely it is the right time for him to come now, when the Romans rule us so harshly, and we are a sad and unhappy people. One day he will be born, Mary, and that will be a wonderful day for the people of Israel."

2: MARY AND THE ANGEL

Mary had often heard tales of the angels that had appeared to the men and women of olden times. She loved listening to these stories, and, like you, she often wished that she could see an angel.

One day, when she was alone on the hills, she was suddenly dazzled by a bright light shining near to her. She looked up in astonishment – and there, standing in the middle of the brightness, was a tall and beautiful being. His wings overshadowed him, and he looked at Mary out of eyes that shone with happiness.

Mary was half-frightened. She knew the wonderful being was an angel, and although she had always longed to see one, she

She gazed at him in wonder

had never really thought that she would. She gazed at him in wonder, trembling a little at his strange beauty and brightness.

God had sent his angel to tell Mary something wonderful, something she could hardly believe was true.

"Hail, Mary!" said the angel. "I bring you great news. You are to have a little baby son, and you shall call him Jesus. He shall be great, and shall be called the Son of the Highest. He shall reign over his people for ever, and shall be greater than King David. Of his kingdom there shall be no end."

Mary gazed up at the angel, full of amazement and wonder. "But how can this thing be?" she asked. "I am only a girl. I am not even married yet."

"The little baby shall be the Son of God," said the angel. "He shall be a holy child. And behold, I will tell you yet another strange and wonderful thing. Your cousin Elizabeth, who is an old woman, shall have a baby son too, for with God nothing is impossible."

Mary's heart was filled with joy when she heard all these wonderful things. She was to have a baby of her own, the little King she had so often heard about! She, the little village-girl, was to have the holy baby, and not any royal princess. She could hardly believe it was all true.

But there was the shining angel in front of her. It must be true. Mary spoke to him again, humbly yet proudly.

"Behold the handmaid of the Lord. I am ready to do whatever he wishes."

Then the angel went away, and the dazzling brightness faded. For a little time Mary stayed alone thinking of all that the angel had told her. It was glorious news. The great King that God had promised was to lie in her arms, he was to be her own baby son. Mary's thoughts grew dreamy as she wondered what he would be like, and she tried to imagine how he would become King.

Mary wanted to tell someone about the angel, and what he had said. She thought she would go to see her old cousin Elizabeth. Elizabeth would listen and believe.

So, that springtime, when the sun shone warm and golden, and the flowers sprang bright beneath her feet, Mary went to the hilly country towards the south, where her cousin Elizabeth lived. She had to walk, and it took her a long time, but she was so happy that she did not feel at all tired.

The birds sang around her. The flowers looked up, brilliant in their springtime colours. The lambs frisked in the fields and on the hills. Everything seemed young and fresh and new. Mary sang as she went and thought many, many times of the little baby that the angel had promised to her.

She came at last to her cousin's house. Elizabeth came to greet her, her face full of gladness. She held out her arms to Mary.

"I know your news!" she cried. "How fortunate you are, Mary – the happiest woman in the world! How proud I am that you, the mother of the coming King, should come to see me. And I, too, have news for you. Although I am an old woman, I am to have a baby son of my own."

"I know," said Mary. "The angel told me, Elizabeth." Then something filled her heart and she had to sing. Words came to her, and she sang a new and wonderful song that people sing in church to this day.

"My husband, Zacharias, saw an angel when he was in the temple one day," said Elizabeth. "He told him that I was to have a baby, and that his name was to be John. My son and yours will be little cousins, Mary – Jesus and John. Stay with me for a while, and we will often talk together of the wonderful things that are to happen."

So Mary stayed with Elizabeth for three months, and then went back to her home. She was happy as she went back, for Joseph the carpenter had asked her to marry him and be his loving wife. She would soon go to his house and make it a happy home for him.

Joseph knew Mary's secret, for an angel came to tell him. He stood beside Joseph's bed one night and spoke to him as he slept, so that it seemed to Joseph that he was in a dream.

The angel told Joseph that God had promised to send the little baby King to Mary. "His name shall be Jesus," he said. "Marry Mary, Joseph, and take her to your home."

So Joseph the carpenter went to Mary. He told her how the angel had come to him in his sleep. Mary was glad that Joseph knew her secret, and she told him that she was ready to marry him. Then, when the baby King came, they would see Him together.

And so Mary married Joseph, and went to his little house as his bride. She heard him at work in the mornings as she went about the house. She went to see the things he was making, and he was proud to show them to her. He was glad to have the gentle, kindly girl as his loving wife, and loved to hear her singing about the house.

No wonder Mary sang as she worked. No wonder her eyes shone with gladness as she walked in the hills that summer and autumn. She waited and longed for the coming of the baby son that the angel had promised.

"His mother will not be a royal princess. She will be the wife of a village carpenter," thought Mary. "He will not be born in a great palace, with many servants around him. He will have only me to look after him, bath him and sing to him. I will love him and tend him. No little prince shall have more love than I will give him, the little Son of God, my own baby boy."

And so Mary waited patiently for the coming of the little King, whilst Joseph hammered and sawed in the little house among the hills. The summer went by, and the autumn. Soon the time would come to welcome the holy child.

3: THE JOURNEY TO BETHLEHEM

Now, that winter, men came into the towns and villages and put up big notices. The people crowded round to read them, and the children wanted to know what they said too.

"The Roman Emperor, Cæsar Augustus, has commanded that everyone shall pay him a tax," said their mothers and fathers. "A tax is a sum of money. We shall have to pay it."

"Where do we pay the money?" asked the children. "Who will come to collect it?"

"We all have to go to our own town and register our names to pay the money," said the grown-ups, sadly. They did not want to have the trouble of journeying to far-off towns, nor did they want to pay money to a foreign king. But their country had been conquered, so they had to do what they were commanded.

Joseph and Mary talked together about having to register their names and pay the money. "We belong to the family of David," said Joseph. "Our home-town is really the city of Bethlehem, not Nazareth, where we live now. Our family lived at Bethlehem, so we must go there to register and pay our taxes."

"Must we go?" said Mary. "It is winter-time and cold. Bethlehem is a long, long way for me to walk, and just now I don't feel very strong. Oh Joseph, must we go?"

"We must," said Joseph sadly, for he knew that the long journey would tire Mary. They could not get to Bethlehem for three or four days, for it was a long way away and was on a hill. "You belong to the family of David, so your home-town is Bethlehem, too. We must both go. Don't worry, I will look after you."

"But I am sure I can't walk so far," said Mary.

"You shall ride on the little ass," said Joseph. "Then you will not be so tired. I will lead the ass, and you shall ride. Come, we must get ready, for we must pay the tax in good time."

So the next day Mary got herself ready, and Joseph cleared up his work-shop and fetched the little donkey. He saddled it for Mary and helped her up. She had packed up food for them to eat on the journey. If she had felt stronger, and it had not been such cold weather it would have been lovely to ride through the hills.

They set off. Many other people were on the roads too, for everyone had to register their names so that nobody could shirk paying the tax to the Roman Emperor. Those who still lived in their home-town were lucky, for they did not need to travel. But those who had left the place where their families had been born and had lived for many years had to do as Mary and Joseph did, and set out on a journey.

"Poor Mary! How tired she looks," Joseph said to the friends they saw on the roads. "What a pity it is such a long way to Bethlehem!"

For some days and nights Mary and Joseph travelled over the little roads that led to Bethlehem. Mary did not like to go too fast. Joseph walked steadily along, leading the patient donkey.

"Are we nearly there?" asked Mary. "I feel so tired."

"Look, Mary – do you see that little town on the hill?" said Joseph, stopping the ass and pointing up the hillside. "That is Bethlehem. We shall not be long now."

"It will soon be night-time," said Mary. "Oh, how lovely it will be to find a place to lie down in. Joseph, there seem to be a great many people going to Bethlehem. How can they all find room?"

"We will go to an inn," said Joseph. "I know of one. We will go there, Mary, and you shall have a quiet room to yourself, and a fire to warm your cold hands. Let me feel them. Only a little while longer, and you will be safe and warm."

Mary smiled at him. Joseph was tired too. He had had to walk, whilst she rode – but soon they would be at the warm, welcoming inn, and then nothing would matter.

They went up the steep, winding roadway. It seemed endless to Mary, and now the night fell and darkness came. At the top of the hill she could see the twinkling lights of Bethlehem. If only they were there! The wind was cold, and the weary donkey stumbled every now and again. Poor Mary had never felt so tired in her life.

At last they came to the town. It seemed full of people, for a great many had arrived there to put down their names as they had been commanded. Mary looked about her anxiously.

"Joseph! Where is the inn? Let us find it quickly and go there. I feel ill."

"There it is," said Joseph, and led the little donkey to where an inn stood by the wayside. Lights shone from it, and it seemed very welcoming to Mary. The noise of many voices came from inside, and it all sounded very cheerful and merry.

"You shall soon be warm and safe," said Joseph, and he called for the inn-keeper. The man came to the door and held up his lantern to see the travellers.

"Have you room for us?" asked Joseph. "My wife is ill and very tired. We have been travelling for a long time."

"My inn is full," said the man. "There is not a sleeping-place to be had! People have been coming into the town all day – if you had been earlier I could have taken you, but now there is no room at the inn."

"No room!" said Joseph, in despair. "But what shall I do for my wife, then? I must find some place for her. See how tired she looks!"

"I can't help it," said the inn-keeper. "If I had room I would take you. But there is no place for you here."

He swung his lantern upwards, and looked at Mary by the wavering light. He saw her white, patient face, with its great, tired eyes, and he was filled with pity, for he was a kindly man.

"Would you like to rest in the stables?" he asked, suddenly. "I have a cave at the back of the inn, in the hillside, where my oxen sleep. There is room there, if you don't mind straw to lie on, and the smell of the warm animals around you. I could have one of the stalls swept out for your wife, and put down some clean straw for her."

"Yes, Joseph, I will rest there," said Mary. "I can go no farther to-night."

The inn-keeper called one of his servants, and it was not long before part of the stable-cave was swept out and new straw put down. Mary went into the cave and lay down thankfully. She was in great pain and was very tired. It was wonderful to lie down on the soft straw and rest.

Joseph tended her lovingly. He brought her hot milk to drink. He put down a folded rug for a pillow. He took off his cloak and hung it over the open doorway to keep out the cold wind. He was anxious when he saw Mary's white face, but still she smiled up at him.

The oxen stamped in the stalls nearby. The little donkey, who had been stabled with them, munched hungrily at his supper. The warmth from the animals' bodies stole round the cave, and Mary felt warm too. She smelt the smell of the oxen, and saw their breath steaming by the light of the lantern that the innkeeper had hung in the stables. It was a strange place to sleep in for the night, but Mary did not mind.

And, that night in Bethlehem, the little baby King was born – born in the stable, with the patient oxen standing by, and the wakened doves cooing in the roof. The lantern shone with a flickering light on the tiny baby in Mary's arms.

"The little Son of God is here," said Mary, and she kissed the tiny face with her heart full of love and joy.

4: THE BABY JESUS

It was wonderful to have the little child in her arms. He seemed so small, and his hair was like the down on a little bird's breast. His skin was as soft as flower-petals, and his tiny nails like little pink shells.

"I have no cradle for him," said Mary. "There is nowhere for the little child to lie. Fetch me the clothes I have made for him, Joseph. I brought them with me in case he was born whilst we travelled. I will put them round him."

In those days babies were wrapped round and round with a linen cloth. The mothers called them swaddling-clothes, and they were the first a baby wore. Joseph gave them to Mary, and she wrapped the baby in his first swaddling-clothes. She crooned to him as she tended him, and was very happy when his little hand found her finger and closed round it tightly.

"I know where we can put the child," said Joseph, who wanted Mary to lie down and sleep.

"Where?" asked Mary. "He cannot lie on this rough straw."

"We will put him in a manger full of soft hay," said Joseph. "That shall be his cradle."

So the tiny child was laid in the manger, and fell asleep in the sweet-smelling hay. He was so small that even the manger seemed big; Joseph pulled the hay around the tiny body, and then went to make Mary comfortable on her straw bed. She was happy as she lay there. God had kept His promise. He had sent her His beloved only Son, and she was His mother. What did it matter that He was born in a dark stable, and had only a manger for a cradle?

Mary fell asleep, Joseph sat beside her, watching that nothing should disturb her. The baby slept peacefully, and did not waken when an ox stamped restlessly on the ground. The shadows jumped here and there as the lantern-light wavered, and the wind shook Joseph's cloak where it hung across the cave-entrance.

That was the first Christmas, when the little Christ-Child was born. We keep Christmas because it was His birthday. Because of the tiny child sleeping in the manger we rejoice at Christmas-tide, and remember what happened nearly two thousand years ago in the dim stable where the oxen stood.

The Son of God, the Great King, had come into our world. Joseph knew and Mary knew – but no one else in the inn guessed that the King of Kings lay sleeping in the hay. No bells rang to proclaim His birth. Nobody knew of the Holy Child in the city of Bethlehem.

The angels in heaven knew! They had been keeping watch over the city, and they knew that the little Son of God had been born. They wanted to tell somebody, because the news was so wonderful. They must come into our world and spread the good tidings, no matter how startled the people might be!

5: THE SHEPHERDS ON THE HILL

There was no one awake in the city of Bethlehem for the angels to tell, but on the hillside outside the town there were shepherds watching their sheep.

Sometimes wolves came at night and took the lambs; so when it was dark the shepherds took it in turn to guard their flocks. That night they were gathered together, their cloaks wrapped closely around them, for it was cold.

They were talking about the crowds of people who had come to the little city of Bethlehem. All day they had seen them walk up the hill, and it had been quite an exciting time for these quiet country-men.

"The Roman Emperor will get a great deal of money from us," said one shepherd. "How I wish we were a great nation, as we used

They saw a bright and beautiful angel

to be. But one day we shall be, for our promised King will come."

"Yes, he will come," said another shepherd. "I hope he will be born in *our* life-time. I would like to see him before I die."

As the shepherds spoke together, looking round every now and again at their quiet sheep, a strange thing happened. A great light appeared in the sky and all around them. It was so bright that the shepherds were afraid. What could this light be that shone in the darkness of the night?

They looked around fearfully, and then they saw a bright and beautiful angel standing near to them, in the midst of the light. He shone like the light itself, and his voice, when he spoke, was like grand music.

"Look!" said a shepherd, clutching the arm of the man next to him. "Look! What is this?"

"An angel!" whispered another, and one by one they all fell upon their knees. Some covered their faces, for the light was dazzling. Then the angel lifted up his voice and spoke gladly to the trembling shepherds.

"Fear not; for behold I bring you good tidings of great joy, which shall be to all people. For unto you is born this day in the city of David a Saviour, which is Christ the Lord. And this shall be a sign unto you – you shall find the babe wrapped in swaddling clothes and lying in a manger."

The shepherds heard these words in the greatest amazement and wonder. What news was this? The King was born, and was not far from them. The angel had told them so.

As the wondering men gazed up at the angel with his great shadowy wings, another strange and beautiful thing happened. The darkness of the sky gave way, and there appeared all above and around the angel a great crowd of shining beings, rejoicing in the news. The world seemed full of angels, all singing in joyful voices.

"Glory to God in the highest, and on earth peace, goodwill toward men! Glory to God in the highest, on earth peace, goodwill toward men!"

The shepherds watched and listened in the utmost wonder. Never had they seen such a sight; never had they imagined such a host of wonderful beings. The whole sky was full of them, and the country-side echoed with their joyful voices. It seemed as if all the angels in heaven had come to the quiet hillside to tell the news.

Then slowly the brilliant light faded, and the glory disappeared. The angels vanished and the darkness slipped back. Only a faint echo of their voices could be heard, "Glory to God . . . goodwill toward men . . ."

Then that too faded away, and the stars shone down as before, twinkling in the darkness of the night. A dog barked, and somewhere a bird called.

For a little while the shepherds said nothing. They waited to see if anything else was going to happen. One of the dogs crept up and put his nose on his master's knee. He had been frightened when the great light came. The shepherd patted him and spoke in a low voice.

"Did you see them too?"

Then the other shepherds spoke, at first in low voices, half-fearfully, then more loudly as they grew excited.

"They were angels! We saw angels, and heard them. Did you see the first one, who was near to us, with his great wings and shining eyes?"

"I was afraid. But it was all wonderful!"

"At first I thought I was dreaming. But no one could dream a dream like that."

"Why did they come to *us*? What was it the angel said? I was so astonished that I hardly heard."

"He said that the Saviour had come! He said that he was born in the city of David this very nght."

"The city of David! Why, that means the town of Bethlehem, up on the top of the hill. We've been watching the travellers go there all day long."

"The promised King is born to-night! Can it be true? He must be a tiny baby then."

"Of course it is true. The angels would not come to us and tell us the news if it had not really happened. I expect the whole town was asleep, and we were the only people awake. How wonderful! Did you see the whole sky full of bright angels? Did you hear what they said? They sang it over and over again. I shall never forget it."

"Can't we go and find the little King? It would be wonderful to see him."

"What! In the middle of the night?"

"Why not? The angel said we should find him there, and surely he would not have told us that, if he had not meant us to go and find him? I shall go, anyway."

"But how can we find him? We don't know where he is. He may be in any of the houses in the town. We can't go knocking at every door and asking if there is a new-born baby there."

"We can do anything to-night! We are men to whom angels have come. Surely we were meant to find the little King and worship him? I shall take him one of my new-born lambs."

"But where can we find him? He can't be in one of the houses, because the angel said he was in a manger. Nobody puts a baby in a manger if it is born in a house. It would have a cradle."

"Yes – he did say in a *manger*. The little King, son of the Highest, in a manger! Can this be true?"

"We shall only know if we go to see. We must go, and go at once."

"The baby must belong to one of the travellers. Maybe they went to the inn and it was full. I know that once before the inn-keeper let his stable out for travellers to lie in. We'll go there."

The shepherds rose up together. They pulled their cloaks round them, for the wind was cold. They left all but one of their dogs to guard the sheep. One shepherd picked up a new-born lamb and put it round his neck to take to the little King. Then, with the dog following close at their heels, they went up the dark hillside, still marvelling at what they had seen and heard, eager to find the little new-born babe.

Sometimes they looked up into the starlit sky to see whether any angel would appear to guide them. But the night was dark and still now. They went up the hill towards the town. They knew where the inn was, and soon they saw the dark building standing beside the way.

They stopped and whispered together. Should they knock at the door and ask the inn-keeper if there was anyone in the stables? Would he be angry at being awakened?

"Look! There is a light burning at the back of the inn!" said a shepherd, suddenly. "It is from the cave where the inn-keeper stables his oxen. There must be someone there. Let us go and see."

So, treading very quietly, the little company made their way round the inn to the stables in the cave. Across the entrance hung Joseph's cloak. The shepherds peered over it anxiously, not knowing quite what they would see.

Then, by the light of the dim lantern, they saw exactly what the angel had told them they would see. A tiny baby, wrapped in swaddling clothes, lay fast asleep in a manger.

"Look! There is the baby!" whispered a shepherd. All of them gazed into the dark stable. They saw Mary asleep in her bed of straw. They saw Joseph sitting nearby, guarding her. But always their eyes went back to the tiny child sleeping so peacefully in his bed of hay.

"He is in his swaddling clothes, just as the angel said," whispered the shepherds. "How wonderful that the Christ should be here, before our eyes – the child that brought all the angels out of Heaven to tell us the news!"

The dog whined a little. He could not understand all the happenings of the night – the brilliance of the angels, the singing voices, and now this unusual journey up to the town, when they should have been guarding the sheep. His master put his hand on his head to hush him. But the noise of the whispering voices had roused Mary, and she awoke.

"Who is there?" she said, and Joseph went to see. He was astonished to find a group of shepherds outside with their dog. They pressed round him, telling him of the angels and what they had said. They went into the cave-stable, and looked at the sleeping child with awed and wondering eyes. Mary lifted him from the manger, and the shepherds knelt before him.

"The angels came and told us we should find the little Son of God dressed in swaddling clothes, lying in a manger," said the shepherds, and they told Mary all that had happened that night. Mary marvelled at their tale, as she held her sleeping child. The dog gazed at the baby too, and the oxen, surprised at the visitors in the night, turned their big heads and looked on with great wide-open eyes.

The shepherds went at last. One of them left the new-born lamb with Joseph as a present for the little child. The dog followed the shepherds out into the night, his tail wagging because he knew that now they would go back to the fields again. They spoke eagerly to one another as they went down the hill. It had been wonderful to see the angels, but it seemed even more marvellous to them to have seen the Christ-Child himself. All that the angel had said had come true.

"What will people say when we tell them to-morrow?" said the shepherds. "They won't believe us! To think that *we* were told the news first. What was it the angel said? We must get the words exactly right. 'Fear not; for behold I bring you tidings of great joy, which shall be to all people'."

The shepherds soon knew the words by heart, for they repeated them so often. The next day they told everyone what had happened, and their fields were soon full of children, marvelling at the story, eager to hear it over and over again. And Mary, in the cave, soon became used to seeing shy eyes peeping at her and the sleeping child.

She looked down at the little head and thought about everything that had happened. She thought about the shining angel who had come to her nine months before. She thought of her old cousin Elizabeth, who now had a beautiful baby boy called John. She thought of the angel who had appeared to Joseph in a dream. She pondered everything in her heart, and wondered what kind of child the tiny baby would grow to be.

Before long the people who had slept in the inn went home again, and Bethlehem was no longer full. It was possible to find lodgings, and Joseph soon set Mary and the child on the little ass and took her to a comfortable house where she might stay. She looked round at the old stable when she left it, remembering the awed and excited shepherds.

"Angels came from Heaven to sing at your birth," she whispered to the tiny child. "I had only a manger to give you for a cradle – but you had angels to welcome you into this world."

6: THE THREE WISE MEN

Now, in a distant land, far away to the east where the sun rises, there lived some wise men. These men knew and understood the stars. They said that the stars told them the thoughts of God. They were sure that whenever a new star appeared it was God's way of telling them that something great was happening in the world below.

One night the wise men thought they saw the faint light of a new star in the sky. They pointed it out to one another, and watched it carefully through the night. The next night it was brighter. The third night it was so bright that its light was more brilliant than all the rest of the stars put together.

"Now what does this great star mean?" said one wise man to another. "God has set it there, in that place, to tell of something wonderful. What can it be?"

They looked in their old books, and they read about the great king who was one day to be born into the world to rule over a mighty kingdom. He was to be king of the Jews. Perhaps this star meant that he was born, for the star seemed to hover over the kingdom of Israel, where the Jews lived.

"We must go to see," said the wise men. "If he is born, then we must take him presents and worship him. The old books say that he will be the greatest king the world has ever known."

So they called their servants and bade them get travelling camels ready, and pack everything they should need. "We will take rich presents for the little king," they said. "We will take food for ourselves. We will take tents to sleep in at night, for we are a great way from the land of Israel."

Their servants got everything ready. They too were to go with their masters. The wise men were so rich that they were like kings or chieftains in their own country, and they never travelled without a crowd of servants behind them. Whilst the star still shone bright in the sky they set off, their big camels striding fast through the night.

For many days and nights the wise men travelled on their camels. They had to pass over deserts, but the spreading feet of their camels found it easy to tread the shifting sand. Always the star shone before them at night and seemed to guide them. It was a wonderful sight to see in the big dome of the sky.

At last the travellers came to the land of Israel. They went to Jerusalem, where the Jewish kings lived, and arrived on their camels at the gates of the great palace itself.

"We are here!" said one of the wise men. "It has been a long journey for us – but now we shall see the new-born king."

Now at that time the king of the Jews was a wicked man called Herod. The Romans allowed him to remain king of the Jews, but he was always afraid of having his power taken away from him. As soon as he feared anyone he killed him.

His servants ran to see who these strange and magnificent visitors were at the palace gates. They bowed themselves down before the wise men, and asked them to come before their master, King Herod.

So, into the presence of the wicked king went the wise men, their turbans and robes seeming strange and unusual in the court. They bowed to Herod, and asked him a question that roused his fears and jealousy at once.

"Where is he that is born king of the Jews?" they said. "We have seen his star in the east, and are come to worship him."

"What do you mean, the king of the Jews?" said Herod, his face darkening. "I am the king. This is my palace to which you have come. What star have you seen in the east?"

The wise men explained. "The star cannot mean you, King Herod, for it has only just appeared, which means that another king of the Jews had been born, a great one, greater than any that have gone before."

Herod's heart was filled with anger and fear. Who was this new-born king? He had not heard of him. Where was he? If only he could find him, he could kill him. But it would be foolish to let the wise men know this. So Herod smiled craftily at the magnificent strangers, and said that he would do all he could to help them.

"I have many wise men in my own court," he said, "and we have wonderful old books in which are kept the sayings of clever Jews who lived long ago. They, too, prophesied that a great king would come one day. Perhaps this is the king you mean. I will try to find out for you in what town he is to be born, then you can go and find him."

Then Herod called for his learned men, and asked them if they knew anything of a great king who was one day to rule over Israel. "Tell me what you know," he commanded.

"We know of that king," said the learned men. "It is written down in the old books that he will come."

"Do the old books say where he is to be born?" asked Herod.

One of the learned men stepped forward with an old scroll in which were written the sayings of the men of olden times.

"Here is a saying that may tell us the birth-place of the king," said the man. "Listen, o king!" Then he read from his scroll. "'But thou, Bethlehem-Ephratah, which art little to be among the families of Judah, out of thee shall one come forth unto me who is to be ruler in Israel'."

"Bethlehem!" said Herod. "So the little town of Bethlehem is to be his birth-place. Go there, my friends, and seek the new-born king."

"Where is this town of Bethlehem?" asked the wise men. "Is it far?"

"No, quite near," answered Herod. "The people of Bethlehem often walk down the hillside and then up to Jerusalem. You will soon get there."

"Then we will go at once," said the wise men. They were so eager to see the new-born king that they did not wish to stay a moment longer in Herod's court.

"Wait!" said Herod. "I want you to do something for me. I, too, am anxious to see this little new-born king and worship him. When you have found him, come back to me and tell me about him. As soon as I know where he is in Bethlehem I will go to him and kneel before him."

It seemed to stand right over the hill town of Bethlehem . . .

"We will come back and tell you," said the wise men. "The town is not big, you say, so it will not take us long to find him. Farewell!"

They called their servants and mounted their camels. With their harness jingling, and the sinking sun flashing on their jewelled turbans the wise men set off once more, glad to think that their journey's end was so near at hand.

As the sun set the great star shone out in the sky again. It lighted up the whole night with its brilliance, and seemed to stand right over the hill town of Bethlehem.

"The star is pointing the way for us," said the wise men one to another. "See how it stands right over Bethlehem. Surely the little king must be there."

The shepherds on the hillside stared as they saw the company pass by in the light of the strange star. Villagers hurrying home gazed in amazement at the strangers on their camels. Why should grand folk like this journey up the road to Bethlehem?

When they got to Bethlehem they asked whether there was a new-born baby in the town.

"Yes," said the woman they asked. "Do you see that house yonder? You will find the babe there with his mother."

The wise men looked at the little house. The star seemed to stand right over it.

"It must be the house," said the wise men. "The star is pointing it out to us. Let us go there."

And so they went to where Mary was, with the little child. She was greatly astonished to see three such magnificent strangers coming before her, and when they knelt down and worshipped the baby on her knee, she gazed at them with wide eyes.

"The little king of the Jews!" said one of the wise men. "We have come to him at last. Let us give him the presents we have brought him."

In those days the presents that were given to kings were such things as jewels, sweet-smelling scents and wonderful spices. It was these things that the wise men had brought to Jesus, for was he not a king? Then he must have kingly gifts! The servants brought in the boxes from the saddle-bags of the camels, and laid them down before their masters. The wise men undid them, and took out the presents.

"Here is gold," said one.

"Here is frankincense," said another.

"Here is myrrh," said the third.

Mary gazed at the wonderful presents, and held the baby

close. She loved him so much and he belonged to her. Yet it seemed as if he belonged to Heaven and the angels, to magnificent strangers who came to worship him, and to the shepherds in the field. They knew him and loved him too. He belonged to the whole world.

The wise men went, for it was night. They left behind them the boxes, and Mary took out the presents again and again, marvelling at their beauty and sweet smell.

"The strangers said that they had seen King Herod to-day," Mary told Joseph. "It was the king who told them that our baby would be found here in Bethlehem. They are to return to him to-morrow to tell him where our little Jesus is."

The wise men went to stay at the little inn for the night, for it was now late. Their camels were stabled in the cave where Mary had stayed on the night when Jesus was born. The same doves cooed there. The same oxen stamped their feet. The wise men took the best rooms the inn had, and prepared themselves for sleep.

"To-morrow we will return to Herod's palace and tell the king where the baby Jesus lives," said one.

But they did not do this, for in the night God sent them a dream. When they awoke, the wise men looked at one another.

"I was warned in a dream not to return to Herod's palace," said one.

"I too," said another. And the third one nodded his head. "We will return home another way," he said. "We will depart this morning, and we will not journey through Jerusalem, in case the king has set his soldiers to watch for us."

So they left Bethlehem and went back to their country by another way, rejoicing in their hearts that they had found the holy child and had given him their presents.

"He will indeed be a wonderful king," said the wise men to one another. "Such a star as his, that stopped over the very house where he lay, has not been seen before."

"King Herod will try to find him," said one wise man. "Perhaps we should have warned his mother, when God sent us the dream saying that we must not return to Herod."

"If God warned us, then he will warn the child's mother," said one of the others. "It was told me by the inn-keeper that Herod is a wicked king. He cannot wish the new-born king any good."

Meantime Herod was waiting impatiently in his palace for the return of the wise men. When would they come? How long they were in returning!

7: A SAD DAY FOR BETHLEHEM

Herod was angry when the wise men did not return to him at once. He thought maybe they would spend one night in Bethlehem, but surely they would come back to Jerusalem the next day?

When they did not appear, Herod sent his servants to find out what had happened. They went to Bethlehem, and soon learnt that the magnificent visitors had departed another way, and must by now be a good way on their journey.

Then Herod fell into one of his furies, and raged violently against the wise men.

"I will send swift horsemen after them. I will take them captive. They shall tell me where this new-born king is to be found."

But the wise men were too far away to be overtaken. Herod's servants told him this and trembled, for their master was a wicked man, and no one knew what he would do when he fell into one of his insane furies.

"I must find this baby," raged Herod. "I shall know no peace till I have found him. He shall be killed! I will not have any little king growing up in my kingdom. I will find him and kill him."

But nobody knew where the baby lived, nor did they know how old the baby was. A baby might be one week old or one year old. The wise men had not told Herod the age, and indeed they had not known it. Herod asked his learned men, but they did not know either how old the baby was.

"It is impossible to find this child and kill him," said one of the men.

"I know a way," said Herod slowly. "I know a sure way of killing this child, this new-born king. Bring the captain of my soldiers here. I have work for him to do."

Herod was wicked, and wicked people are always cruel. Herod's eyes gleamed as he thought of his plan. "I will have every boy-child under two years old killed in Bethlehem!" he thought. "Every single one! Then the new-born king will be sure to be killed among them, for not one shall escape."

He gave orders to the captain of his soldiers. They were terrible orders. "Slay every boy-child under two years of age in the city of Bethlehem and the villages round about," he commanded. "See that none escapes."

You may wonder how anyone could be so cruel, but evil and cruelty go always hand-in-hand. The captain saluted and turned to go. He gave his soldiers their orders, and the men left the palace to go up the hillside to the city of Bethlehem. They had done many wicked things by Herod's orders, but there had been nothing so terrible as this.

They soon arrived in Bethlehem. The people there were amazed. Why should Herod's soldiers go there? The children flocked out to watch them – and then, seeing a baby boy carried by a little girl, one of the soldiers slashed out with his shining sword – and the child was dead. The little girl ran screaming indoors. "Mother! Oh, Mother! Our baby, our darling little baby!"

Then people knew that something terrible was happening, and they ran to bring their children indoors. The soldiers were shouting for the boy-babies, and trembling mothers tried to hide them.

"Herod's command!" shouted the soldiers, and they broke down the doors and strode into every house, hunting for the poor little children. A weeping and wailing rose on the air, and the whole city was in an uproar.

The soldiers did their work well. They killed every boy-child under two years old in Bethlehem and round about. Then, sheathing their cruel swords they rode down Bethlehem hill to Jerusalem, and went into the presence of their master King Herod.

"Every baby boy is slain," the captain reported, and Herod nodded, well pleased. Now he was safe. Now the little new-born king, heralded by a star, visited by wise kings from the east, was dead. He would not take Herod's throne. Herod had been stronger and cleverer than any new-born king of the Jews!

The king did not hear the sobs and wails of the poor mothers in Bethlehem. He did not see the white, fearful faces of the older children, watching in terror lest the soldiers should come again. He cared for nothing but himself and his power.

8: HOW JESUS ESCAPED

The baby Jesus was not in Bethlehem when the soldiers came, so he was not killed with the others. He was far away, quite safe.

When the wise men had left Mary, the little family went to bed and fell asleep. As Joseph lay fast asleep an angel came to him in his dreaming and stood beside him, even as one had done before he was married to Mary. Joseph looked up at the angel, and listened to what he had to say. The shining being brought a strange message to Joseph in the middle of that quiet, dark night.

"Arise!" said the angel. "Arise and take the young child and his mother, and flee into Egypt, and stay there until I tell you to come back again; for Herod will seek the young child to destroy him."

Joseph awoke and sat up amazed and wondering. The angel had gone. It was a dream – but a dream sent by God. Joseph awoke Mary and she opened her eyes.

"Mary! I have seen an angel in my dream," said Joseph, in a low voice, for he did not want to wake the baby.

"What did the angel say?" asked Mary.

"He said we were to take little Jesus and escape with him into Egypt," said Joseph. "The angel said that Herod would send here to kill him. Those strange men who came here last night with such wonderful presents must have said a great deal about Jesus to Herod. We must go at once."

"Now? In the middle of the night?" said Mary, astonished.

"Yes," said Joseph. "We must do as the angel said, and he bade me take you at once. Get the child ready, Mary, and some food. Pack up our things, and I will go to find our little donkey. He shall carry you and the baby. Make haste, for I feel we have no time to lose."

Joseph dressed and went out into the yard. He found the little donkey, who was most surprised to see his master in the middle of the night. Joseph saddled him and brought him to the door.

Mary packed up their few things hurriedly. She took food and packed that too. They would need it on the journey, for it would take two or three days. Then she picked up the sleeping baby, and held him closely in her arms. Her heart went cold when she thought of the wicked King Herod. He had killed so many people already in his life. He must not kill her beloved little child.

Then, silently, in the dark of the night, the four of them – Joseph, Mary, little Jesus and the patient donkey – went along the quiet roadway, out of the city of Bethlehem. They went quickly, and only stopped a short time to eat and drink, for whilst they were in Herod's kingdom they were in his power. They must get to Egypt as soon as possible, then they would be safe.

And at last they arrived there and settled down to wait until God should tell them it was safe to return again to their own country.

So, when Herod's soldiers came to Bethlehem with their sharp swords, Jesus was not there. A great number of lovely babies were slain, but Jesus was not among them. He was far away in another land, tended by his loving mother, who waited patiently for word to come so that she and Joseph might return once more to their own people.

Then Herod died. The wicked king had to give up his kingdom and his throne, and go to face his God. Joseph knew of his death, for again an angel came to tell him.

"Arise," said the angel, "and take the young child and his mother, and go into the land of Israel; for they are dead which sought the child's life."

Then gladly Joseph arose, and saddling the little donkey, took Mary and the boy back into his own land. Jesus was no longer a baby. He looked around at everything he passed as they went on their way. There was no hurry this time. They were not escaping from evil.

But when Joseph had travelled a good way he heard that Herod's wicked grandson was on the throne. His name was Archelaus, and he was as full of evil as his grandfather.

"Maybe he too will want to kill the child," Joseph said anxiously to Mary. "Do you think it is wise to go back to Bethlehem? I know it is the city we belong to, because we are both of the family of David, and Bethlehem is David's city – but there might be danger for Jesus."

"It is near to Jerusalem," said Mary. "Jesus could go to school there. And surely such a holy child should be taken often to the Holy City? Oh, Joseph, what is the best thing to do?"

"Perhaps I shall have another dream," said Joseph. "I am sure we ought not to go to Bethlehem, but I don't know where else to go. I would rather not be in any part of the king's country."

Then God sent Joseph another dream, and told him to go and live in the land of Galilee.

"Joseph, Nazareth is in Galilee," said Mary. "Shall we go back there? We both know it well, and we have friends there. Let us take Jesus there."

And so the little family journeyed to the town they knew so well, Nazareth, set on the green hillside. The little white houses shone in the sun as they went up to the city. This was to be Jesus' town, the place where he played and worked, thought and dreamed, where he grew from a small child into a thoughtful boy, and from a boy into a wonderful man.

9: THE LITTLE NAZARENE

Jesus lived in a little house made of sun-dried brick. Joseph white-washed it every year, and it shone in the sun. It was very much like all the other houses in the town, and Jesus liked to pick it out from the cluster of white buildings whenever he came home up the hillside.

Joseph set up his carpenter's shop there. The sound of hammering and sawing came often to the ears of the little boy, and he liked to see his father at work. He liked to hold the heavy hammer, and sort out the big and little nails. He liked to dip his hand into a pile of soft sawdust.

Sometimes Mary took him for walks up to the top of the hill. There was a lovely view from there, and Jesus could see the blue sea beyond further hills. In the spring and summer there were thousands of gay flowers everywhere, shining blue and yellow and pink. The anemones grew wild on the hills, and it was lovely to pick bunches of them for his mother. The little boy noticed everything – the beauty of the deep heart of the crocus, the sudden joyous call of a bird, the trembling dewdrop on a blade of grass, the sweet playfulness of the new-born lambs in the fields.

Jesus liked to go down to the well with his mother to fetch the water in the big stone crock. There was nearly always somebody else at the well, and it was fun to talk and hear the news. [You could see the same old well at Nazareth to this day, if you were able to go there.] When he was older Jesus would fetch the water by himself. Every drop had to be carried to the house, for there were no taps to turn on and off like ours.

There was no bright electric light in the evenings, either. If the Nazarenes wanted to see after dark they lighted a queer little lamp that stood on a stand. It had a wick floating in oil, and this gave a dim light to the room. Jesus liked the flickering shadows as he listened to the old stories his mother told him at night.

Mary told him many tales that you know very well. She told him the story of how God made the world. She told him about the Garden of Eden, and the angel with the flaming sword. He knew about Noah and the ark, and he liked to think of all the animals there. When he looked at the rainbow that sometimes came in the sky he remembered Noah, and how God had promised to set the brilliant bow in the heavens as a sign that he would not destroy the world.

The little boy noticed everything . . .

Joseph told the little boy stories too. He told him about David and the fight between him and the giant Goliath, and of how the little shepherd-boy became a great king. He told him of the strong man, Samson, who had strength as great as a lion, and of Daniel, who went into the lions' den, and was unharmed.

Both Mary and Joseph told Jesus of God, and taught him his prayers. All the Jewish children were taught to pray to God and to obey his commands. Jesus thought a great deal about his Heavenly Father as he wandered over the countryside.

We know what kind of a boy Jesus must have been, because of the wise and kindly things he said when he was a man. He told so many stories of sheep and lambs that he must often have watched them himself as a boy, and have carried the little lambs in the crook of his arm. He must have done many of the things that country boys did then, but he saw them with clearer eyes, and loved them more than most boys.

He watched the men sowing seed in the springtime. He saw them scatter it with their hands, and watched the seed fall in many places – some by the wayside where people trod on it, or the birds ate it – some on stony ground where it could not grow – some in the hedges where it was choked by weeds – and some on good ground where it grew and flourished and brought the farmer a rich harvest.

He lay in the fields and watched the birds and the little animals, hearing their songs and calls, seeing them go about their own little affairs, and he loved them. He went some nights to sit by the shepherds' fire in the fields, and to hear them talk. That was an exciting thing to do. The fire was lighted to keep away prowling wolves or a mountain lion, and it was easy to imagine some big animal skulking in the dark shadows. It was a good feeling to guard the helpless sheep and lambs.

Sometimes lambs were lost, and Jesus went with the shepherds to find them. He would toil over the hillside for hours to find one little lost lamb, and how he rejoiced when at last he found the frightened little thing, bleating piteously.

Jesus saw and remembered all these things, and when he was a man he put them into stories that he told to the people. You will read some of these later on in our book. In them we can see little bits of his childhood, the childhood of a wise and kindly boy, whose clear eyes saw deep into the heart of things, and who longed to help his friends, and his enemies too, and to bring them some of the wisdom and love that grew steadily in his heart.

10: TWELVE YEARS OLD

Jesus was an only child for a while, and then brothers and sisters were born in the little house at Nazareth. Jesus was the eldest, and he helped his mother to look after the smaller ones. He loved them, as he loved all children. He played with them, made little wooden toys for them in the carpenter's shop, and told them tales.

Jesus could always be trusted to do a thing when he was told. He could always be trusted to guard a smaller child carefully, or to go an errand for his mother. Sometimes he would carry a table or a bench to a customer for his father, and people would welcome the clear-eyed boy, and get him to talk to them.

"He's not quite like other boys," they would say to one another. "Have you noticed? He thinks for himself. He's so kind, too. You can always go to him for anything. Joseph and Mary are lucky to have a boy like that."

The other boys sometimes thought that Jesus was strange. He troubled himself about things they never thought of, and he would never agree to any injustice or unkindness. He was strong and courageous, and sometimes he would speak his mind so plainly about things that they were astonished. Most people accept what they are told, and do not think things out for themselves, but Jesus always used his own clear mind to reason things out. Then he would say what he thought, and it would be so sensible and wise, and yet, maybe, so different from what everyone else thought, that his friends would look at him in surprise, and say: "You always think differently from everyone else, Jesus! You're a strange boy."

Jesus went to school. He learnt his lessons and especially the law of God, which all Jewish children had to learn very carefully. A great many teachers had written down this law, and it had become very long and very difficult. In the law was set down what God wanted his people to do, even in such small things as washing a plate.

Jesus learnt the law and thought about it. Into his heart came the thought that surely God must care more about whether a man was kind and just, than whether he washed a dish in a certain way, or wore certain kinds of clothes. He looked round about his friends, and saw how they tried to obey all the little commands of the law, and how difficult it was for them to remember everything.

"If only we could have a simpler law, if only the people knew that it is much more important to be kind to one's neighbours and to forgive one's enemies than it is to wear our clothes a certain way!" the boy thought. "There is John now, who lives down the hill, and is so careful about all the little commands of the law – and yet he is an unjust man and hard to his children. Then there is old Hannah, whom everyone scorns because she forgets to keep the little commandments – but who could be more generous to her neighbours than she is, sharing everything she has, and giving her last penny to help another?

Surely, when God looks into the hearts of John and of Hannah, he will know that Hannah's kindness is worth more than John's outward show? I wish I could tell everyone this. It is a thing they should know. There are other things, too, that seem wrong to me, and yet that seem right to everyone else. I must think about them, and pray about them. One day I shall see everything clearly, and perhaps I shall have the words to tell everyone what is in my thoughts."

Every year Joseph and Mary went a long journey to the Holy City of Jerusalem, where their beautiful Temple stood. The Jewish people kept a certain feast or holiday each spring, just as we keep Christmas or Easter, and at this time they liked to go to Jerusalem and join in the great meetings and services there. Each year Jesus said to his mother: "Let me go with you! It is lonely without you at home. It would be so lovely to set off with you and everyone else."

And when he was twelve years old, his mother called him to her and said: "This year, Jesus, you *shall* come with us. You are old enough now to join the church and to become one of its members. You have learnt the law, and you must now promise to keep it. You shall go with us to the Temple this year."

This was great news to the boy. He had always wanted to go to Jerusalem, for he had heard a great deal about it, and he wanted to see the beautiful Temple there.

Besides this, there was the great excitement of setting off on the long journey, for it took some days to travel to Jerusalem. Many people from Nazareth would be going and it would be wonderful to walk along strange roads, and to camp at night by the wayside. Jesus was happy. It was something to look forward to.

"Only two more weeks," he thought. Then, "Only one more."

In the carpenter's shop . . .

And at last there were only two days, then one day – and then the great day came. Some of Jesus' own friends were going too, and they talked together about the road they would travel.

"We go down the hill and across the plain, first," said his friends. "There will be millions of flowers out. We'll look out for old spear heads in the fields there. Last year James found one sticking up from the ground. It might have belonged to King David when he fought his battles over those very fields."

"We cross the River Jordan," said a boy. "And we've got to be careful not to go through the country of those horrible Samaritans My father says they are dreadful people."

"Why?" asked Jesus. "They can't all be wicked or horrible! There must be some good ones. How does your father know? Has he ever been to the country of the Samaritans?"

"No. But everyone knows they are dreadful," said the boy, impatiently.

"What everyone knows isn't always true," said Jesus, and he began to think about the Samaritans, and to put them into a story that came into his head. But the boys thought no more of it and went on to tell one another the way they would go to Jerusalem. It was a great adventure to them.

Joseph and Mary made preparations for the journey. They were excited too, for it was a wonderful change for them to leave their quiet home and journey so far away to the great city of Jerusalem. Joseph set his shop in order, and hastened to send out the things he had just finished. Mary tidied the house and piled the bed-rugs on the bench at the back of the room.

"I am glad you have learnt the law so well," she said to Jesus. "I really think you know it better than any of the other children. I am happy that you will be able to join with us in worshipping God at our church. Oh Jesus, Jerusalem is a wonderful place. You will see it first from the top of the Mount of Olives. When we get there you will look across a valley, and there, below you, will be the city of Jerusalem with its towers shining brightly in the sun."

The little family set off. They made their way down the hillside, and joined with their friends. Everyone was joyful.

"We're going at last!" said the children, and they ran to walk with Jesus. "The day has come at last. We're really going to Jerusalem!"

11: JESUS IS LOST

Everyone enjoyed the long walk in those early spring days, over the hills and plains to Jerusalem. There were flowers everywhere like a brilliant carpet. The sun shone warmly, and the birds sang in every bush. The children enjoyed every moment. Sometimes they ran ahead, climbing the hills before the grown-ups did, longing to see what was over the top. Sometimes they lagged behind, watching the lambs frisking in the fields, or the men at work. There was always something to see.

When night-time came the children were tired, and so were their parents. They set up camps by the roadside, in a spot sheltered from the wind. They made fires and cooked simple meals. The children helped. Jesus went to look for bits of wood to feed the fire. It was good to smell the food cooking, and to watch the smoke curling away.

Darkness came and the light from the fires twinkled under the night sky. Voices murmured together, and then someone started a grand old hymn. It went from camp to camp, and everyone joined in, children too.

Those were good days, as the company journeyed to Jerusalem. When they came near to the city some of the children, who had never been before, and who, like Jesus, were to join the grown-ups' church for the first time, became silent, wondering what it would feel like to enter the Holy Temple, and to know that God was very near to them.

"There is the Mount of Olives," said Mary, as they rounded a bend in the road, and saw a hill in the distance. "You will see the gleaming towers of Jerusalem from there!"

The first sight of the Holy City was wonderful to the children. They stood on the Mount of Olives and looked silently at the Holy City in the distance. Jesus tried to pick out the white walls of the Temple. There God dwelt, his own Heavenly Father.

They entered the city with hundreds of others who had come to share the Feast of the Passover there. Then followed some happy days for Jesus. He was taken to the Holy Temple, where he felt that God was very near to him. He heard beautiful music and much singing. He was made a Disciple of the Law, and was told by the wise men in the Temple that from that day he must count himself grown-up – he must do as his father and mother did – keep all the laws, all the rules, all the feasts and fasts of his religion. Jesus knew these laws well. He had learnt them all at school, and he had thought about them for a long time.

Then the time came for everyone to walk back home again. The Feast was over. People must get back to their daily work.

Mary packed up everything they had brought with them It was not much. Joseph took the packages, and they set off to walk home. Everyone was leaving the city now.

"We shall not see some of our friends again for many a month," said Mary. "It has been good to meet so many people and to hear their news. But it will be nice to be in our own home again."

Little groups of friends and relations walked together, talking of all that had happened during the week. Mary kept looking for Jesus, but she did not catch sight of him all day. She thought he must be with the other boys in front somewhere. He was a grown boy now, and she could not expect him to keep with her all the time.

"He will come and join us when we make camp for the night," she thought. So neither she nor Joseph really worried about him.

Darkness fell, and the little companies halted to make camp. Mary watched for Jesus to come and help her. She listened for the sound of his voice, but she did not hear it among the shouts of the children near.

"Joseph, where is Jesus?" said Mary, anxiously. "I have not seen him all day."

"He will come soon," said Joseph. "I will go and ask our friends in front if they have seen him. Perhaps one of the boys will know whom he has been walking with to-day."

But nobody had seen Jesus. "He was not with us," said one company. "We have not seen him at all," said the children.

Nobody had seen Jesus that day on the road. Then Mary and Joseph began to be really troubled, and they turned back to seek for him among the people behind them on the road. But he was not there. Everyone shook his head. "No, we have not seen your boy. The last we saw of him was in Jerusalem. Perhaps he did not know that you had started."

Mary said they must go all the way back to the Holy City. "He must still be there," she said. "Oh Joseph, we must find him quickly!"

So back to the Holy City went Mary and Joseph, their hearts full of anxiety. They went to the house where they had stayed, but he was not there. Nobody had seen him. Nobody knew where he was.

For three days Mary and Joseph stayed in Jerusalem, looking

for Jesus. It was a big city, and there were many places to search. But still they could not find him.

"Maybe he is in the Temple," said Mary at last. "You know how he loved being there. Perhaps he has gone back there."

So the two of them went to the Temple – and there they found Jesus. He was not playing in the city, he was not watching the hundred and one strange sights to be seen there. He was in the Temple, trying to find out all he could about God and his commands.

He had gone to the wise and learned men there, the men who knew more about the difficult Jewish laws than anyone else. He was asking them questions – questions that no one had ever asked them before. He was making those wise men think deeply. And they in their turn, amazed at the wisdom and knowledge of the twelve-year-old boy, were asking him questions too.

Jesus answered the questions gravely and wisely. The learned men looked into his clear eyes and marvelled at all he said. It seemed as if Jesus knew the law as well as they themselves did, and some of the learned men wondered where such a small boy could have gained so much wisdom.

Jesus had never before met clever men such as these. He wanted to know so many things. He poured out questions that had puzzled him and listened intently to the answers. Perhaps there had come to him for the first time the idea that one day he might help the world, that one day he might have something to say that people would long to hear. He felt within himself the power for doing good, the urge to possess all the knowledge he could get, so that he might turn it into good and simple words of wisdom to help the common people.

It was no wonder that the wise men listened to him and marvelled. For a long time Jesus stayed with them, standing in their midst – and then he saw Joseph and Mary, looking at him with surprised and troubled eyes. Mary went to him and put her arms round him, almost weeping with relief.

"Son!" she cried. "Why have you behaved like this to us? Your father and I have been seeking for you everywhere, full of sorrow."

"Did you not know where I would be?" asked Jesus in surprise. "Did you not guess that I would be here in God's Temple, my Father's house, learning things about Him that I must know?"

Joseph and Mary were not quite sure what he meant, but they were so glad to have found Jesus again that they said no more. He went home with them, telling them on the way some of the questions he had asked the wise men, and what they had answered him. Mary looked at this wise little son of hers, and listened. She stored all he said away in her heart, and when she was alone she thought of his sayings with wonder and awe.

But wise and wonderful as the Christ-child was, he was still only a boy not yet grown, and he saw that he must obey his parents in all things, and not cause them worry. So he settled down once more in Nazareth to the quiet life he knew so well. He did as he was told, helped his parents as much as he could, and loved his brothers and sisters tenderly. Much knowledge could be gained in the beautiful courts of the Temple at Jerusalem, but wisdom and understanding could only grow slowly in the quietness of his heart. This he understood, and was content to live with his family in the quiet town of Nazareth.

12: JESUS GROWS UP

When Jesus went back home with his father and mother, after going to Jerusalem, he found that he was treated from that time more like a grown-up person than a child. He did not go to school so often, but helped his father in his shop. Jesus was to be a carpenter like his father, and must learn his trade.

So, to the boy's delight, he was allowed to try his hand at many things in the shop, and Joseph let him make some of the simpler things for the customers. He let him mend some of the broken tools and furniture that the villagers brought to him, and soon people found that the carpenter's son was very thorough and dependable.

Jesus had plenty of time to think his own thoughts as he hammered and sawed. He grew older and more thoughtful. He saw that his ideas were different from those of the people around. Soon he became sure that his ideas were simpler and wiser than those of others, but it was not yet time to prove this. He was so young.

He saw that goodness and kindness, justice and unselfishness were the things that really mattered. He knew that cruelty and greed, spite and unkindness were evils to be fought. If he was going to preach this to others, he himself must be sure to see that only good things were in his heart. He must cast out of himself all that was bad. So, in those years of boyhood and youth, Jesus taught himself the lessons he was afterwards to teach others. He grew into a wonderful man, full of love towards everyone, full of understanding, longing for the day to come when he might go out into the world and preach the marvellous things he knew to all the men and women he met.

His goodness showed in his face, as goodness always does. It shone from his eyes and in his smile. It turned people's hearts to him so that they trusted him and loved him. It made the little children run to him and slip their hands in his.

And now Jesus was a man. The years passed slowly by, and soon he was known as Jesus the carpenter of Nazareth, a man who did good work and was always just and fair. Then Joseph died, and Mary turned more and more to this wonderful son of hers. She did not always understand him, for although she was his mother, and loved him dearly, Jesus had wisdom that came from God, and some of his sayings puzzled her simple mind. But always she knew that he was the Holy Child of God, heralded by angels, and often she wondered what his real work in life would be.

Mary needed Jesus when Joseph died, and so he stayed with her in Nazareth, going about his work as usual. He could not leave his mother whilst she wanted him by her – but when the right time came, he would go.

The time did not come until Jesus was a grown man, nearly thirty years old. Then he knew for certain that he must leave the city of Nazareth and go out into the world. He had his Heavenly Father's work to do now – not carpentering, but preaching. Now was the time when he could go to the people and tell them the great thoughts that had been in his heart and mind for so long.

And so at last Jesus left Nazareth, and went to do the work that God had sent him into the world to do. He was to found a great kingdom, a kingdom of love. He was the Saviour, the Messiah, the Son of God come down to earth, the greatest man the world had ever seen.

13: JOHN, THE COUSIN OF JESUS

Now, some time before Jesus left Nazareth, there began to be talk of a strange preacher called John, who preached beside the River Jordan. This was Jesus' own cousin, the son of Elizabeth, Mary's cousin, whom she had stayed with after the angel had come to her when she was a girl.

John was a little older than Jesus. He had lived a lonely life in the country, and, like Jesus, he had thought deep thoughts and wanted to tell them to others. So one day he left his work and went out to preach.

John was used to a simple life, and he did not worry about his food or his clothes. He took a cloak of camel's hair for himself and wore that. It would not wear out easily. Round it he tied a leather girdle.

"He looks like a wild man!" said the people to one another. "What can he have for food? He has no one to look after him."

"He finds the honey of the wild bees," said a boy. "He told me so. And he eats those insects called locusts, when they come."

John was a wonderful preacher, quite fearless. He was called John the Baptist, because after he had told people to stop doing wrong things, and do good instead, he wanted them to show that they meant to, and to let him take them into the River Jordan and baptize them.

"If I baptize you and make you clean in the water, that will be a sign to everyone that you will put away evil things and wash your hearts clean, so that good things may come there," said John. So, when they had listened to him, and were sorry for their wrong doings, hundreds of people went to John to be baptized, and to promise to try and do right.

"John the Baptist is wonderful," the people said to one another. "He is not afraid of telling anyone when they do wrong, not even the proud Pharisees and Sadducees who set themselves up to be so good and great."

"He told them they were snakes," said one. "I heard him. He said they must turn from their evil ways like the rest of us. They were very angry."

"He says we are all to be kind to one another and share everything with those who are poorer than ourselves," said a woman. "And did you hear what he said to the tax-collectors? He said they were only to take from us the rightful sum of money, and not demand more and keep it for themselves as they usually do."

"He spoke sternly to the soldiers who went to hear him preach, too," said a man. "He told them not to be cruel, and not to accuse anyone wrongly. He is a great man, John the Baptist. Do you think he can be the Saviour who has been promised to us by God?"

Then many people began to say that perhaps John was the Son of God. But when they asked him, he shook his head.

"No," he said. "All I can do is to baptize you with water, and prepare you for the coming of the real Saviour. He is mightier than I, and I am not worthy even to do up his shoes."

Then the people wondered among themselves about the new Messiah, who should be greater than John the Baptist. "I shall know him when he comes," said John.

One day Jesus came. He had left Nazareth and had walked to the River Jordan, for he had heard of the wonderful new preacher. John saw him coming towards him, and he stood marvelling at the beauty and goodness that shone from Jesus' face.

"Behold!" said John, with awe. "Behold the Lamb of God!"

"I come to be baptized by you," said Jesus.

"You have no sins to wash away! It is I that should be baptized by you," answered John. But he baptized his cousin,leading him into the waters of the river.

Jesus' heart was full of joy as John baptized him, for he felt that God was very near to him and loved him. As he came up out of the water, a strange thing happened.

The sky seemed to open and a bright light shone out. The Spirit of God came down in the shape of a dove, and seemed to rest on the head of Jesus. And there came a voice from Heaven, saying: "This is my beloved son, in whom I am well pleased."

14: JESUS AND SATAN, THE PRINCE OF EVIL

When Jesus was baptized, and knew that he was to be the Saviour, God's own son sent down from Heaven, he needed to think about all that it meant.

He had heard so much about the Saviour who was to be king of the Jews. How strange that he, a village carpenter, should be the man chosen by God to do His work. Jesus felt within him a great power. He felt that he could do things that no one else could. It was a great and wonderful thought, and he had to think about it by himself.

So he went away into the lonely countryside and began to plan what he would do. He would put all his deep thoughts into simple words for people to hear and understand. He would tell them stories to make things easier for them. He would comfort the sorrowful, and try to heal those who were ill. God would help him in everything.

Jesus wandered about the countryside, lost in his thoughts. He forgot to eat for many days. He was filled with joy to think that he had been chosen to fight and conquer the evil things of the world, and to bring into it a kingdom of love.

But the Prince of Evil, Satan, was not pleased to see the Son of God in the world, planning to fight evil with goodness. So he came to Jesus and whispered thoughts into his mind, to tempt him away from the life Jesus had been planning to lead. He knew that Jesus was just beginning to feel the wonderful power of God within him, the power that could help him to work miracles that seemed like magic, the power to heal ill people, and make the dead live again.

So, knowing that Jesus was now feeling very hungry, Satan put a thought into his head. "Why don't you turn the stones over there into bread? Surely the Son of God can do that?"

But Jesus would not. Satan whispered another thought, and, as if a dream, took Jesus to the topmost pinnacle of the Holy Temple at Jerusalem.

"Look!" said Satan. "You are high above all the city – but because you are the powerful Son of God, you could throw yourself down, and yet come to no harm. Is it not written in the Bible that God's angels shall have charge over you to guard you, and they shall bear you up in their hands lest at any time you dash your foot against a stone? Then throw yourself down, and that will prove to yourself and to everyone else that you are the Son of God."

But Jesus would not do anything so stupid. Then Satan tried for the last time. He took Jesus to a high mountain, and, in a moment of time, showed him all the kingdoms of the world lying before him.

"See!" said Satan. "Great kingdoms and great power await you, if you use your gifts for me instead of for God. I can give you all these if you will but follow me and worship me, as other men do. It will be hard for you, a carpenter's son, to become a great king, merely by preaching and praying. But I can soon make you one, if you will be my servant."

But again Jesus would not be tempted. He turned upon the Prince of Evil, and said: "Get you behind me, Satan. You know that I should worship the Lord my God, and serve only Him."

Then Satan knew that he was defeated, and he fled away. A great gladness came into Jesus' heart when he knew that he had conquered Satan for ever. Now he could use his power and his gifts for God, and, whatever happened to him, however difficult his life might be, he would belong to God only, and could guide others aright.

Then it seemed to Jesus as if angels came to him and cared for him, and he was glad.

15: THE FIRST FRIENDS OF JESUS

Jesus left the lonely countryside and went to the land of Galilee. He meant to begin his work at once. He wanted to preach to everyone who would listen. He wanted to tell them the wonderful things he knew.

He knew that he must have someone to help him. He would need to teach others, so that they could carry his words far and wide. So he must choose his first friends, his disciples, who would believe in him and teach the same things as he did.

Jesus walked one day beside the beautiful Lake of Galilee. He watched the fishermen at work, and in one boat he saw two brothers. Their names were Simon and Andrew, and they were good fishermen. Jesus liked the look of these men. He felt sure he could trust them, and that they would learn from him.

So he called to them across the water. They looked up from their nets and saw Jesus. There was something so beautiful about him that they could not take their eyes off him.

"Come with me," said Jesus, "and I will make you fishers of men!"

Simon and Andrew did not know what he meant. They could not know that Jesus meant them to try and catch men to bring them into the Kingdom of Love. But although they did not know what he meant, they did know that they must leave everything, and go with him.

They pulled their nets into the boat, took the oars and rowed for the shore. They jumped out and went to Jesus, asking him eagerly what he meant.

A little way along, Jesus saw two other brothers in a boat with their father. They were busy mending their nets. Jesus called to them, too.

"Come with me!"

Then the two brothers, James and John, came to the shore and followed Jesus. They and the others were his first real friends, who were to help him all his life and afterwards too. He chose eight more, but these four were closest of all to him.

One of them was very lovable. This was Simon. He was brave and he was kind, but he could be untrustworthy too. No one was ever sure of Simon.

"He could be wonderful," people said, "but somehow he just fails."

He called to them across the water

But Jesus knew that Simon was the right man for him. He looked at him and said: "Your name is Simon, but I shall call you Peter."

"Why shall you call me that?" said Peter, in surprise.

"Because Peter means a Rock," answered Jesus. "One day you will be as steady as a rock, Peter, and the kingdom I am going to build will depend a great deal on you. You shall be Peter, a rock."

Jesus chose twelve friends altogether, men who loved him and understood his words so that they themselves could go out into the countryside, when they were not with him, and preach to the people. They were his twelve followers or disciples, and a very happy company, following their beloved Master wherever he went.

16: JESUS BEGINS HIS WORK

And now Jesus really began his great work. He went about the country-side talking to everyone. He preached in the churches. He found simple and beautiful words for the great thoughts he had in his mind. Everyone understood him, even the little children. He made nothing difficult.

"The Kingdom of God is at hand," said Jesus. "Do wrong no more, but believe in the gospel, the good news I bring you. God is your heavenly father, and He loves you. Trust Him and fear nothing. Turn from evil and do good. Then happiness will come to you, and great joy."

The people listened to Jesus, and looked at him. They could see that he was goodness itself. They crowded round him, loving him, wanting to hear every word he said. His fame went all round the countryside.

"Have you heard Jesus preaching? It is wonderful. You know who he is, don't you? He is the son of Joseph, who was a carpenter of Nazareth. Come and hear him to-day. The things he says are easy to understand, and he will comfort you and bring you joy."

So more and more people went to hear him preach. The churches were filled when he spoke there, and the fields and hillsides were crowded with eager listeners if he preached in the open air. The people felt that Jesus knew what he was preaching about, for they felt sure that he himself was as good as he wanted them to be. When he looked down at them with love and understanding in his eyes, everyone wished to be the same, and to love others.

"This man speaks as if he really knew and meant what he says, and not as our other teachers speak," the people said to one another.

And then Jesus began to use his wonderful power of healing. He could not bear people to be sad or in pain. He was loving and tender-hearted, and quick to feel when people needed his help.

He knew there was a great and unusual power within him. He could make sick people better by touching them, or by speaking to them. This was a wonderful gift, and very soon the whole countryside was full of wonder and excitement at the things Jesus did.

"He does not only preach! He heals those who are ill! Truly he is the Son of God! I was there yesterday when he made a poor man quite well. He is a wonderful man."

"He heals both soul and body! This is surely the Messiah, the Saviour. Leave your work and come with me to hear him. Just to touch the robe he wears is something to remember."

Thus it happened that wherever Jesus went a crowd followed him. Some of them hoped to see him do wonderful things, miracles that seemed like magic to the people. Some of them wanted to hear him preach. The children went because they loved him and knew that he was the most wonderful man they had ever seen.

And some went because they were ill and hoped to be made better. In those days doctoring was not so marvellous as it is now, and there were many, many things that no doctor could cure. Nowadays, no matter how ill anyone is, there is always hope that he may be cured in one way or another because of the great discoveries that have been made about our bodies and how they work. But in those far-off days, when a person was seriously ill, very little could be done for him.

So it happened very often that people suffered for years, and would have given anything to be cured and to have back their health and strength. It was a wonderful thing to them suddenly to hear of this man Jesus, whose magic touch could bring healing. No wonder they flocked to him, or begged their friends to take them.

"He *might* heal us," said the sick people to themselves, and a great hope came into their sad hearts. "Anyway, we will go to him. If only we can get near enough to ask him for help! There are so many people round him every time."

17: THE NOBLEMAN'S SON

Now there was a nobleman who lived in Capernaum, and he had a little son. His father loved him with all his heart, and petted him. He gave him servants to wait on him, and brought him toys and sweets. He thought his small boy was the finest in the whole world.

One day the child fell ill. The nobleman looked at him anxiously He took the boy on his knee and felt his hot hands and hot forehead. The child didn't want to play. He didn't want to eat.

"We must call in the doctor," said his father, and a servant was sent to fetch one. The doctor ordered the child to bed, and told the nobleman what to give him to eat. He must be kept very quiet, then he would soon get better.

But the little boy didn't get any better. When his father went to see him, he seemed worse. His eyes were too bright. He tossed from side to side and moaned. His father gathered him up in his arms and held him close. What was he to do? Perhaps another doctor would know better than the first one!

So he sent for another, and yet another. He was a rich man, and he did not mind how much he spent on his beloved little son. It made his heart go cold to see the child lie so restlessly on his bed, tossing in pain.

The nobleman spoke anxiously to the doctors. "The child doesn't seem to be any better. He seems worse. He won't – he won't – oh, surely he won't *die*, will he?"

The doctors looked gravely at the father. They knew the child was dying already. There was nothing they could do.

The nobleman saw what was in their faces, and his heart was full of pain and sorrow. He loved his little son so much. He went into his own room, and paced up and down, wondering what else he could do. And whilst he was there, his servants came in to him.

"Sir," they said, "have you heard of a new and wonderful doctor called Jesus? He preaches and he heals, too. He has done some marvellous things. Couldn't you get him here and ask him to heal the little boy? He will surely die if something is not done soon."

The nobleman looked at his servants and a small hope came into his heart. "I will try *anything*," he said. "Tell me where this man is."

"He is at Cana," said one of the servants eagerly. "Let me go to him with a message, sir. Give me a letter. I will run quickly and bring him back to you."

"No. I will go myself," said the nobleman. "I will beg him to come. He *must* come! Oh, my dear beloved little son, what should I do without you if you died? You are everything in the world to me!"

The man went to take a look at his small boy and then set off to Cana. He went as quickly as he could. If only this preacher, whoever he was, could make his son better! He would give him anything he wanted!

On the way he met others who told him exactly where to find Jesus. They told him, too, that Jesus was not exactly a doctor, but someone who preached a better way of life, a way of goodness and love. The nobleman began to think he must indeed be a marvellous man.

At last he came to the house where Jesus was. He waited anxiously for him to come, hoping and hoping that he would be able to persuade him to go back to Capernaum with him.

Jesus came into the room. The nobleman looked at him, and out of his anxiety and sorrow came the knowledge that this man had enough power and goodness to do good to anyone, well or ill. Always when people were in great trouble they trusted Jesus, and felt his loving power.

"Sir," said the nobleman, urgently, "my little boy is ill in Capernaum. He is dying. Please, please come back with me and cure him. I know you can make him well again. Will you come back with me? I love my son so much."

Jesus wondered if the man had come simply to see him do a miracle. So many people now came to watch for wonders. Then they said they would believe he was the Son of God. Jesus did not want them to believe in him because he was able to do miracles. He wanted them to believe in his preaching and to do what he told them to do.

"You and others only want to see me do miracles," he said. "You will not believe me unless I do something wonderful."

"Sir," said the nobleman, desperately. "I don't want signs or wonders. My child is dying, and I only want you to come back with me and see if you can cure him. Come with me now, or he will die."

Jesus looked at the anxious man, and his heart was filled with pity and love for him. "Don't be afraid," he said, gently. "Your son lives. Go home, and you will find that my words are true."

The nobleman looked at Jesus' grave face, and believed him. His heart was filled with such joy that he could hardly bear it. He left the house and hurried back home. He did not for one moment doubt that Jesus had spoken the truth. He was sure his son was better. Although Jesus had not spoken to the boy, or seen him or touched him, in some way his power had reached the child and had healed him.

As he came near his home, the nobleman saw that his servants were watching for him. They ran to meet him, and their faces were joyful.

"Sir! Your son is well! See – here he comes!"

The nobleman saw his little son coming towards him, helped by a servant. He held out his arms, and the child snuggled into them. "I'm better," he said. "My head is better. I want to play a game with you."

The man caressed the little boy and looked at him with joy and love. Such a gladness filled his heart that he could hardly speak. He pressed the boy to him and looked up at the smiling servants.

"What time was it when the child began to be better?" he asked.

"Sir, he was on the point of death," said a servant, "and then, at seven, the fever left him, and he was better."

"Seven!" said the nobleman, and his eyes shone. "It was exactly at that moment that Jesus said 'Your son lives.' What a wonderful man he is! How I wish you could all have seen him! We must go to hear him preach. We will believe all he says and try to do what he commands. And you, my little son, shall go to hear him too, and you must thank him for what he did for you, although you were miles away."

And so, in that household there were many who loved and believed in Jesus, and tried to do all he said. They told everyone of him, and more and more the people crowded round him to hear his words, and watch all he did.

18: THE MAN BY THE POOL

Not far from the sheep market at Jerusalem there was a curious pool. It was called the Pool of Bethesda, which means the House of Mercy. Round it were built five big porches, and steps led steeply down to the water.

It was a sad place to visit, for in the porches lay many sick people. Some had been ill for years. Some were blind, some were lame, some were paralysed and could not move their arms or legs. They were a sad sight to see.

The pool was fed by a spring that sometimes bubbled up, and then the waters were troubled. The surface ruffled and wrinkled itself. At this time the pool was known to have healing power, and as soon as the poor sick folk nearby saw the waters wrinkling, they tried their best to hurry down the steps to get into it. Those who bathed in the troubled waters first felt much better.

"Surely it must be an angel that comes down to the water and troubles it!" the sick folk said. "We must watch day by day. If only we can bathe in the pool when the angel comes down, we shall be made better."

One of the sick people was a man who had been ill for thirty-eight years. He lay by the pool in one of the porches, watching for the ruffling of the water. But he could never seem to get down the steps in time to share in the healing when the pool bubbled up.

There was always a great excitement when the waters were troubled. A shout would go up.

"Look! Look at the pool! Quick, get down into the waters!"

Then the sick, lame, blind folk would try to hurry down the steep steps to the water, falling, stumbling, helped by friends, all eager to bathe in the pool. Those who bathed in it whilst the spring was bubbling said that they felt much stronger.

Often the sick people had a friend with them so that they might be helped down the steps quickly. But this man who had been ill for so long had no friend to help him. So he had never been able to get down quickly into the water when the time came. He lay there day after day, watching the pool, slowly losing any hope of ever getting well.

Now one day Jesus went to the pool. It was the sort of place he would go to, because he always felt sorry for unhappy people, and wanted to bring them gladness and joy. He passed through the porches, looking with pity at the ill men and women there, and he came to the man who had been ill for so long.

Jesus knew how long the man had been ill. He saw the suffering in his eyes, and was sad for him. He went up to him and spoke to him.

"Do you want to be healed?"

The man looked up in surprise. When he saw the kind eyes of Jesus looking down at him, he began to tell him how hard he had tried to get into the pool when the waters were troubled. "But I have no friend to help me down those steps," he said, "so I am always left behind."

"Rise, take up your bed and walk"

Then Jesus looked at the man, and said a strange thing. "Rise, take up your bed and walk!"

The man was lying on a mattress, where he had lain for years. But when he heard Jesus' words he had no doubt at all but that he could obey. So he rose to his feet, picked up his mattress, and walked. He could hardly believe that he really was walking!

The man was overjoyed and amazed. He could not believe his good fortune, and he was so overcome with joy that he did not notice Jesus slipping away among the crowd. When he turned to thank him, Jesus was not there.

The man went back home through the streets of Jerusalem, marvelling at what had happened. He carried his bed with him, and then he noticed that people were looking at him angrily.

"Of course!" thought the man. "It is the Sabbath day, our day of rest. I ought not to be carrying my bed like this, because it is against the law to do anything that is work or seems like work on the Sabbath. But how can I help it? That wonderful man told me to take up my bed and walk, and I had to obey him."

Some Jews stopped him and spoke to him angrily. "Why do you carry a bed on the Sabbath day? You know it is against the Jewish law."

"Sirs, a wonderful thing has happened to me to-day," said the man, eagerly. "For many, many years I have been ill and have lain on my mattress beside the Pool of Bethesda. But to-day a man came and said to me, 'Rise, take up your bed and walk. And I found I was well, so I did as he bade me, and took up my bed and walked."

"Who told you to do this thing that is against the law?" asked the Jews.

"I don't know," answered the man. "All I know is that he is a wonderful man, and I would like to see him again. He went away before I could find out his name. Don't you think it is marvellous that he made me better?"

But the Jews did not care about that. All they were troubled about was that Jesus had told this man to do something he shouldn't do on the Sabbath day.

Now the man went to the Temple that day to thank God for his good fortune, and in the Temple he suddenly saw Jesus. He went to him at once, and Jesus spoke to him.

"You are healed. Go, and do wrong no more in case a worse thing happens to you."

The man was excited to see Jesus again. Soon he met some of the Jews who had been angry with him because he had carried his bed that day. He ran up to them and pointed Jesus out to them.

"See!" he said. "There's the man who healed me! His name is Jesus."

The Jews called a meeting, and decided that they would send for Jesus. The chief ones among the Jews of Jerusalem were already jealous of him because the people loved him and followed him, so they were glad to have some fault to find with him.

Jesus stood before them, and they accused him of healing people on the Sabbath day. "You know that it is against our law to do any work on the Sabbath," they said.

"My Father does kind deeds even on the Sabbath day, and so do I," was Jesus' answer.

Then the Jews were very angry because he had dared to call God his father. They let him go, but they spoke against him bitterly, and it was plain that they would kill him or put him into prison if they could.

So Jesus left Jerusalem and went to Galilee to teach the people there.

19: THE MAN WHO WAS A LEPER

In the days when Jesus was going about the country, preaching in the towns and villages, there was a man who was a leper. He had a terrible disease called leprosy, which could not be cured. Parts of his body rotted away, and he suffered great pain, and was dreadful to see.

There were many lepers in those days, and people were afraid of them, because they knew that if a leper should touch them, they too would get leprosy. So they drove anyone with leprosy away from their homes, and would not let him live with them.

The poor lepers had a terrible life, for everyone feared and despised them. When they came near any traveller the lepers had to call out "Unclean! Unclean!" So that everyone could avoid them. They lived alone or with other lepers. Their children were forbidden to go near them, and they expected only disgusted glances and harsh words.

Now this man who was a leper had heard of Jesus, and how he cured illnesses. He thought sadly of himself. He had had to leave his family and his friends and go out to live alone in the country-side because of his terrible disease. He would die of it, die alone and uncared-for. If only he could be made well again!

He thought of the happy life he had had before he had discovered the dreadful white spots of leprosy on himself. He longed to be with his friends again, joining in their daily life, instead of living all alone, scorned and despised by any passer-by.

And then the leper saw a crowd in the distance, and wondered why. He dared not go near, but the thought came into his heart that the people might be listening to the wonderful healer. He waited until the crowd went away, and then he went near.

He saw Jesus standing there, and he knew at once that he was the one he was looking for. He knew Jesus could heal him. He had no room for any thought in his heart except that he must tell Jesus he could heal him, if only he would.

So he went to Jesus and knelt down before him, a poor, sick leper with terrible sores.

"Sir," he said, beseechingly, "you can make me well if only you will!"

Jesus looked down at the poor, ugly man, and his loving heart was full of pity for such a poor creature. He put out his hand and touched the leper, a thing that no one else would have done, and spoke to him in his grave and beautiful voice.

"I *will* heal you," he said. "You are well again."

And even as Jesus spoke, the sores healed up, the man's skin grew clean again, and he was healed. He was no longer a leper. He could go back to his family and his friends, he could work and be happy once again.

The man looked down at his body in wonder and joy. It was the happiest moment of his life. He longed to rush to his home and tell everyone.

Jesus saw by the look on his face that the man was eager to tell everyone of the miracle that had happened to him. But he did not want him to go round telling everyone. Jesus found it difficult to preach in the towns when people came crowding round him, eager to watch any wonder that he might do.

So he spoke sternly to the man. "See that you do not say anything to anyone about this. Go to the priest and show him that you are made better so that he will allow you to go home. But be careful not to tell everyone you meet what has happened."

The man left Jesus to go to the priest. He went rejoicing. He looked down at his body every now and again, full of gladness to think that his skin was clean and whole, and that his pain was gone. His eyes shone, and he could not go quickly enough.

Soon he met somebody and shouted to him. "I was a leper, but Jesus cured me! I'm going to the priest."

People did not believe him at first, but when some who had known him to be a leper saw that he was cured, they marvelled. The news went all round like fire.

"The leper is cured! Jesus met him and touched him, and he is cured. He has been to the priest, and now he has gone back to his family. Did you ever hear such a wonderful thing?"

People went to see the man, and he told his story again and again, quite forgetting that Jesus had asked him to say nothing. Everyone was so astonished and filled with wonder that they felt they must go and see this marvellous healer. So when he appeared in the town they flocked around him in such numbers that Jesus knew it was impossible for him to preach there.

He had to leave the town and go into the lonely places of the country-side. But the people came to him even there from far and wide, for now his name was on every man's lips.

20: THE MAN WHO CAME THROUGH THE ROOF

In the city of Capernaum there lived a man who could not move. He was sick with the palsy, and he lived a miserable life, lying on his bed all day long. But he had kind friends who often came to see him and cheer him up.

The man had little to do except think, and he often wondered if his illness had been sent by God as a punishment for wrong-doing. "Perhaps I have sinned against the Lord my God," the man thought. "How I wish that my sins could be forgiven. I am sorry for them. If I had my life over again I would try to do good."

But he could not have his life over again. He could only lie on his bed, unhappy and ill. No doctor could cure him, for he was too ill.

One day his friends told him about Jesus. "This man, Jesus, cured a leper," they said. "A *leper*! Think of that! It's all over the town how he cured him, and scores of other people too. They say he made a nobleman's son well, without even seeing him. And he cured a man who lay by the Pool of Bethesda too. He had been ill for nearly forty years. What a pity he couldn't see *you*!"

The ill man lay and listened to all that his friends said. They did not only tell him of what Jesus had done, but of the fine things Jesus had said. He told people to be good and kind to one another. He told them that their sins would be forgiven them if they were sorry, and tried to do better.

"I wish I could see this man and ask him if he thinks my sins are forgiven," thought the ill man. "I should feel happier lying here without moving all day long, if I thought that God had forgiven me for my wrongdoing."

One day his friends came to him in great excitement. "What do you think!" they cried. "We've just heard that Jesus is here, in Capernaum! We met someone who said he is sure he saw him walking down the street. Wouldn't it be marvellous if you could see him?"

"If only I could go with you and find him!" groaned the man on the bed. The friends talked among themselves for a while, and then one of them went to find out if Jesus really was in the town, and if so, where he could be.

He came back quickly. "Yes! He *is* here! He has gone to a house not far off, and already there are great crowds forming. They say that even the learned men, who know the law from beginning to end, are there to hear him speak to-day. We must go to see him; it's such a chance!"

The ill man looked up with such longing eyes that his four friends knew they must take him too. So each one of them took a corner of his mattress and lifted it. Then, with the palsied man lying on the bed between them, they set off in a hurry to find Jesus.

Jesus had gone to a house which, with other houses, was built round a courtyard. Many houses in his country were built like that. He was in one of the rooms, talking to the people there. There was a crowd in the courtyard outside, pressing against one another, eager to hear his voice and to watch if he did a miracle.

More and more people crowded into the yard until no more could stand there. There were people at the gate of the courtyard too, trying to see over the shoulders of everyone else.

So, when the four men, carrying their friend between them on his bed, came to the house where Jesus was, they could not even get near him! They went to the gate-way, but nobody would let them pass. They stood on tiptoe and saw the great crowd in the courtyard, and they knew that they would never get through the people there, even if they could squeeze into the gate-way. They set the bed down and looked at one another in despair.

"It's no use," said one. "We can't get near."

"We'd better go home," said another. "It's a pity we didn't

Four anxious faces peered down through the hole . . .

hear that Jesus was here before. We might have got into the courtyard then."

The other two looked down at the man on the mattress, and saw that he was bitterly disappointed. He lay there, looking beseechingly up at his friends. If only they could do something!

They could not bear the look in his eyes. "I know what we'll do!" said one.

"What?" asked the others.

"We'll go up on to the flat roof," said the man. "We can easily get there from the outside of the house. And we will dig up the roof and make a hole in it, and let down our friend right in front of Jesus! If he is as kind as people say he is, he won't be angry."

"Would you do this for me?" asked the man on the bed, his eyes shining. "Take me up on to the roof, then."

The four friends carried the man up the steps to the flat roof. The Jews often used the flat roofs of their houses on a hot night, and lay there in the cool breeze, sleeping peacefully. Many of the roofs were made of hard earth, and this roof was no different. The four men laid their friend down gently, and then began to try and dig a hole in the roof of the house!

"We'll tie ropes to the ends of the bed and let him down that way," they said to one another. "Jesus is a good man. He will help our friend; there's no doubt of that."

They dug and dug at the roof, and soon a hole appeared. After that it was easy to break away enough of the roof to let down the mattress on ropes.

Meantime the people in the room below were astonished at the noise on the roof, and even more amazed when they saw a hole appearing, and bits and pieces dropping down. Nobody could think what was happening. Then to their great surprise a mattress was swung slowly down through the hole, and came to rest just in front of Jesus. Four anxious faces peered down through the hole to see that everything was all right.

The man on the bed lay looking up at Jesus. Yes – this was the kind of man who could help him, who could tell him if his sins had been forgiven him, and teach him how to do good.

Jesus saw the men looking down through the roof, and he was touched to think how much they trusted him to help their friend. He looked round at the watching people, and saw that they expected him to do a miracle. But Jesus knew what the ill man wanted more than anything else.

"Man," said Jesus, "your sins are forgiven you!"

Now this was just what the ill man wanted to hear, as Jesus

very well knew, for he was quick to read the thoughts and longings of others. But some of the people around were horrified to hear Jesus' words.

The learned men sat and thought hard thoughts. "This man has no right to tell anyone that his sins are forgiven him!" they said in their hearts. "Only God can forgive sins. This man cannot. How dare he say such a thing."

Jesus looked round and read the hard thoughts in their hearts. "What are you thinking?" he said. "Which do you think it is easier to say to a man like this – 'Your sins are forgiven you,' or 'Rise up and walk'? I will show you that I have power to forgive sins, although you think me just an ordinary man."

Then he turned to the man on the bed and spoke to him. "Arise, take up your bed, and go to your house."

At once everyone looked at the palsied man on the bed. Then, to their great astonishment and wonder, the ill man who had not been able to move for years, rose up, stood on his feet, picked up his bed, and walked out of the house!

Then all who were there in the room, and those who were looking on in the courtyard, and the four men peering down through the roof were filled with amazement and fear. They kept thanking God, and exclaiming at what they had just seen.

"We have seen strange things this day!" they said to one another. "We have seen strange and wonderful things!"

21: THE SOLDIER AND HIS SERVANT

In Herod's army there was an officer who commanded the company there. He was not a Jew, but he liked the Jews, and did all he could for them. He built them a new church, in the city of Capernaum, and maybe Jesus preached in it.

One day his favourite servant fell ill. The soldier sent for a doctor, but he could not cure him. Then the soldier was sad, for he loved this old servant of his, and would have done anything to get him better.

He had heard of Jesus, and he wondered if he could help him. But as he was not a Jew he didn't like to go and ask him. So he went to the chief men in the church he had built for the Jews in Capernaum, and asked them if they would go and tell Jesus about his servant.

They said at once that they would go. They thought it would

be fine to tell Jesus what an important man had sent them, and how good he was to the Jews, and what a beautiful church he had built them. So they went to find Jesus, who was then in Capernaum.

They came to him and told him all about the soldier. Jesus listened – and when he heard of the sick servant he said at once he would go with them. Jesus did not care whether the man's master was great or fine, he only cared about the sick servant and the love his master bore him.

So he set off to the soldier's house with the chief men of the church. But in the meantime the soldier had begun to be sorry he had sent for Jesus.

"He is a great man, and very busy," he thought. "I have no right to make him give up his time and come here. He could make my servant better merely by saying the word. He does not really need to come and see him. I believe that if he could heal him by touching him, he could also heal him by saying that he shall be made better – even though he may not come to my house! I will send my friends to him and tell him this."

So the soldier asked his friends to go and meet Jesus and tell him what he thought, and presently they met Jesus and the chief men of the church, hurrying to the soldier's house. They stopped them and spoke to Jesus.

"Lord, do not trouble yourself to come any further. Our friend has sent us to you saying that he is not worthy for you to come into his house, neither is he worthy to come to you himself. He asks you simply to say the word, and he knows his servant will be healed. After all, he says to his soldiers 'Go!' and they go, 'Come!' and they come, and to his servant, 'Do this and do that.' You too can do the same, and your word will be obeyed. So say the word, Lord, and his servant will at once be healed."

Jesus listened in surprise and pleasure. He turned to the men who were with him and spoke to them.

"No one has put such trust in me before, not even my own people!"

The friends of the soldier went back to the house, when they had given Jesus their message. The soldier came to meet them, his eyes bright with joy.

"You must have given Jesus my message!" he said. "My servant is well again. Come and see!"

22: JESUS MEETS A FUNERAL

There are so many stories to tell of the wonderful things that Jesus did, that it is difficult to choose from them; but here is one of the most wonderful of all.

In the village of Nain there lived a man and his wife. They had a little boy, and they were both proud of him. But one day the boy's father died, and there was no one to look after his mother but him.

"Don't cry, Mother," he said. "I will work for you and look after you. I will keep you safe and happy."

The boy was as good as his word. He worked hard and made his mother very happy. She was proud of him and loved him greatly, for he was all she had in the world.

Then one day he fell ill, and his mother became very anxious. "You don't need to worry, Mother," the lad said, "I shall soon be well again."

But he got worse, and people began to shake their heads and say that he would never get better again. "It's a pity that the wonderful healer, Jesus, is not here," they said to one another. "He might make the widow's son better. It is terrible for the poor woman. First she lost her husband, whom she loved so much, and now her boy is dying."

But Jesus was not in Nain, though he was not very far away. Nobody sent for him, and he knew nothing of the poor widow and her son.

That night the boy died, and the poor mother broke her heart with grief. She had loved him so much, and he had been such a good kind lad to her. Now she had nobody at all. She wept and wailed, and everyone tried to comfort her.

The time came for him to be buried. "You must be brave," said the widow's friends. "You have to walk in the funeral procession. We shall all come, for we loved your boy and are bitterly sorry for you."

The funeral procession set out, carrying the dead boy on his bier. In front walked his mother, crying and sobbing, and with her went her friends, weeping bitterly too. A great crowd walked behind, for everyone was sorry for the mother.

Now Jesus and his disciples were just then coming to the city of Nain. They heard the sobbing and crying, and saw the big procession.

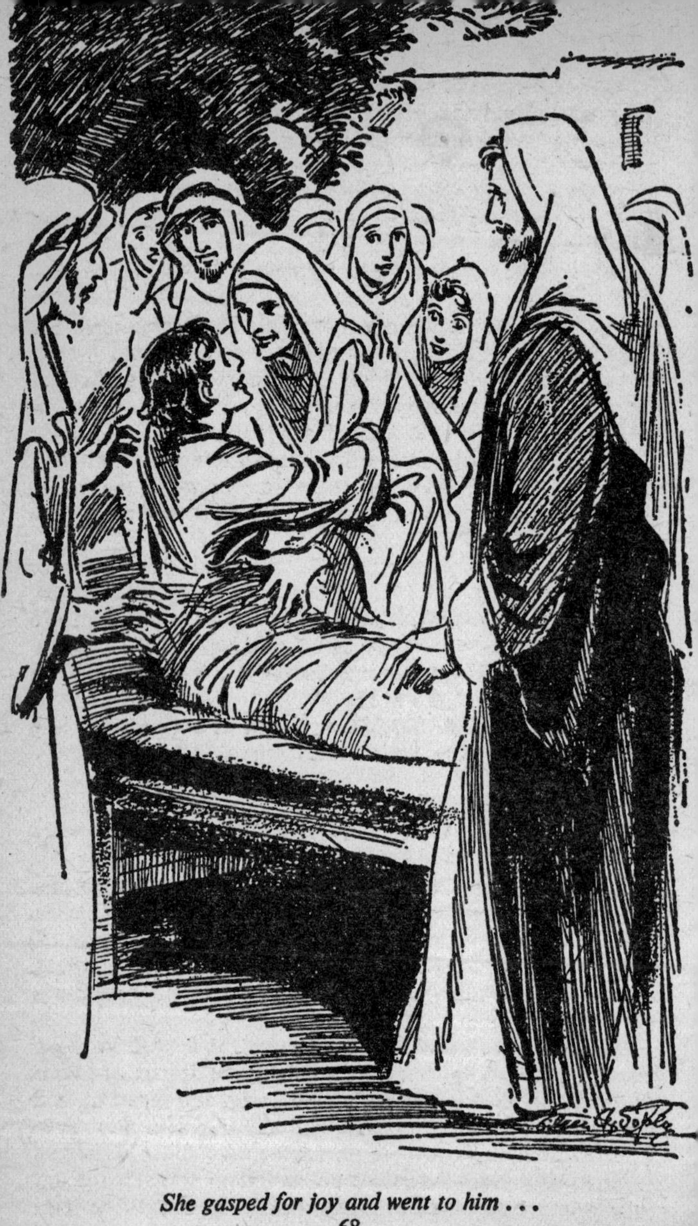

She gasped for joy and went to him . . .

"It is the funeral of a good lad," someone said. "He leaves a widowed mother, and she is broken-hearted."

Jesus saw the poor, bent old mother, and his heart filled with pity for her. He went up to her, and spoke to her.

"Weep not!" he said. Then he turned to the bier on which her dead son was being carried, and touched it. The men who were carrying it set it down, gazing at Jesus.

Jesus spoke to the dead boy. "Young man, I say unto you, arise!"

And the lad sat up, and began to speak. His eyes searched for his mother and he smiled at her. She gasped for joy and went to him, holding her arms out blindly, hardly able to believe what had happened. Not till her boy was safe in her arms, his cheek warming against hers, could she believe that he had come back to her.

The people around could hardly believe their eyes, either. Their sobbing was changed to wild joy. They surged round the widow and her son, they crowded round Jesus and his disciples. Some were half-fearful at the miracle.

"A great man is here with us!" they cried. "God has not forgotten us!"

The widow was happy and her son was happy. The people who had sobbed in the funeral procession were full of joy. Jesus' disciples were glad, too, that their master had been able to bring gladness again to the poor widow.

But the one who was happiest was Jesus. It is wonderful to be made happy, but it is a much lovelier thing to *give* happiness.

23: THE WONDERFUL STORYTELLER

Jesus lived a very full life at this time, for he went about preaching and healing as much as he could. Sometimes, when he had spent a good deal of time touching ill people and healing them, he felt very tired. Goodness flowed out of him when he healed others, and then he had to go away by himself and pray. He needed to get back his strength and his power.

Many of the learned men, and men in high places disliked him because the people listened eagerly to him, and not to them. Some of these men liked to disturb his preaching, and find fault with his sayings. They tried to catch him and trap him into saying something that they could punish him for.

Jesus had to teach the people, and he did not want the precious time he had to be wasted by those who disliked him. So he began to make up stories to tell to the people who really wanted to learn from him.

"Every story shall have a meaning," he thought. "People remember stories easily. My people are simple folk, so I will make my stories simple too, and they shall be about all the things that the people themselves know."

So Jesus made up the wonderful tales that we call the Parables. Each tale has a meaning to it, and most of the people who listened to him understood easily what Jesus meant when he told them the story.

They loved these stories, and were always ready for more. The children could understand them too, and listened as eagerly as the grown-ups. Jesus loved children, and they always ran to welcome him. He set them on his knee, asked them what they had been doing, and looked at the toys they showed him. He was never too busy to welcome them.

One day Jesus walked down the streets of Capernaum and went to the lake there. People saw him on his way and they followed him. There was nearly always a crowd at his heels, watching and listening.

When Jesus came to the shore he saw that a great crowd of people had collected to hear him. He thought he would tell them some of his stories, and perhaps they would remember them and tell them to their families when they got home again.

But it was difficult to talk to the people on the shore, for they pressed round him so closely. So Jesus called Peter and asked him to bring his boat close in to shore. Peter did so, and Jesus got into it.

He sat there, on that sunny day, whilst the crowds sat or stood on the shore nearby. Behind them rose the green hills. On the lake fishermen were out in their boats, fishing, or mending their nets. Everywhere around were the children, peeping and pushing, trying to get to the front so that they might hear better.

And then Jesus began to tell his stories. You shall hear some of them, and guess the meanings he put into them.

24: THE TALE OF THE SOWER

Once upon a time a sower went forth to sow seed. He scattered the seed by hand, first this side and then that.

Some of the seeds fell on the path, where the ground was

trodden hard. The birds in the hedges saw them and came down to eat them.

Some of the seeds fell on stony ground where they had not much earth. They put out little roots, and sent up green shoots. But when the sun came up, the seedlings were scorched, and because they had no earth into which to send deep roots, they withered away.

And some seeds fell among weeds, which grew up and choked them.

But other seeds fell on good ground, where there were no weeds. They grew tall and strong, and when the farmer came to harvest his field, he found that his seeds had given him thirty, sixty or even a hundred times as much corn as he had sown, and he was glad.

The disciples were surprised to hear Jesus telling stories like this to the people. They asked him what this one meant.

Jesus explained to them. "God's word goes out all over the world," he said. "It is written in the Bible, and it is told to us by our teachers. It is like the seed in the story, being scattered everywhere."

"But some people hear God's word and take no notice, and so that seed falls on hard ground and does not grow. Others listen and take heed for a while, but when difficulties come, they give up. They are like the stony ground where the seed grows for a little, and then, because it has no root, dies."

"Then there are others whose hearts are choked by evil. These are like the weedy ground, where good seed cannot grow.

"But lastly there are those who listen to God's word, and remember it, doing all the good they can, and loving others. In their lives you will find kindness and love, and they are the good ground, where seeds bring forth fruit thirty, sixty, or even a hundred times more than was sown."

Jesus told many tales like this one, bringing in the things that his listeners knew so well, and that he himself had watched so often as a boy. Some of the people knew the inner meaning of his stories, and some did not. But all remembered them and understood the simple facts he told.

25: THE TALE OF THE MUSTARD SEED

Jesus told a tale about a mustard seed. He wanted to show people how his kingdom of love could grow.

"The Kingdom of Heaven is like a grain of mustard seed," said Jesus. "A man took this grain of seed, which is one of the smallest of all seeds. He sowed it in his field, and passers-by might have expected only a tiny plant to grow from it. But it grew strong and tall, and at last, in the man's field, that tiny seed grew to be a tree. The birds came and perched in its branches."

So Jesus taught that his kingdom should grow, from a tiny beginning to something so great that it could take in the whole world and everybody in it.

26: THE TALE OF THE FISHERMAN

Jesus put the Kingdom of Heaven into many tales. Here is another that he told to the listening people.

"The Kingdom of Heaven is like the net that a fisherman cast into the sea to catch fish. He and his friends pulled the net in when it was full and heavy. There were many fish there, and the fishermen rowed their boat to shore to sort out their catch."

"They knew the fish that were good and those that were bad. They put the good fish into baskets, but the bad ones they threw away.

And this is how it shall be at the end of the world. The angels shall come forth and gather the good, but the bad shall be thrown away for ever."

27: THE TALE OF THE SHEPHERD AND THE LOST SHEEP

Sometimes people said that Jesus ought not to go about with sinners, and ought not to talk to them and have meals with them as he often did. So Jesus tried to show them in a parable that God loves even bad people and tries to save them from their wickedness.

Why should not he, then, be kind to them and try to bring them into his Kingdom of Love?

"Listen!" said Jesus. "Suppose there is a shepherd with a hundred sheep in his fold. One of the sheep wanders off into the hills, where there are wolves to devour him. Does the shepherd say to himself, 'I have ninety-and-nine sheep safe in my fold, so the lost one does not matter'?"

"No – he leaves the ninety-nine safe, and goes to seek for the little lost one. Will he not seek it until he finds it? And, when he at last finds it, he lays it on his shoulder, and carries it all the way home, rejoicing.

When he comes home, he calls his friends in and his neighbours, and says to them, Rejoice with me for I have found my sheep which was lost!"

"And thus it is in Heaven, for there is more joy over one sinner who is brought again into the Kingdom of Love, than over he ninety-nine good people who are safe."

28: THE STORY OF THE BOY WHO WENT AWAY

Jesus very much wanted to make his people realize how much God loved them, and wanted them in his kingdom, and how he rejoiced when the lost ones came back to him. So he told them many stories about this, and one of the best was the tale of the boy who left his home and went away.

There was once a rich man who had two sons. The father had plenty of servants who waited on him in his house and who worked in the fields. The boys had good things to eat, fine clothes to wear, and money to spend.

The younger son was bored with the life on the farm. He wanted to go out into the world and have a good time. He wanted far more money to spend than his father allowed him.

So he grew discontented and would not work. He idled his days away, and his father was sad to see him. The elder brother did his work well, and always obeyed his father in everything. He did not like his lazy younger brother, and often grumbled at him for not doing his share.

At last the younger son went to his father. "Father," he said, "do you think I could have my share now of what will be mine, and go away into the city? It's so dull here, and I am not happy. I want to leave home. You have my elder brother to do everything. Please let me go."

So the father, seeing that the son would not be happy, gave him his share of the money and bade him good-bye with a heavy heart. The younger son set off in fine clothes, humming a song, his money making his heart light, for now he had more to spend than he had ever had before in his life.

He came to a city and took lodgings there. When the people knew he had plenty of money they crowded round him, and he soon had plenty of friends. He gave wild parties and spent his money freely. He travelled about in the grandest style, going from place to place, gathering friends wherever he went because of his money and the way he spent it.

His money could not last for ever. One day, when he was in a far country, it was all gone, and he had no more. His friends fell away from him as soon as they knew he was poor, and he found himself alone.

"I must get some work to do," thought the youth. But this was not easy. He had not learnt to work hard on his father's farm, and people did not want an idler. Then there came a famine in that land, a great shortage of food. People went hungry and many of them starved. The youth learnt what it was to be faint with hunger for the first time in his life.

At last he found work to do. He was given the job of looking after a herd of grunting pigs. He sat under the trees, watching them all day, so hungry that he would have liked to eat the empty pods and husks that they were given for food.

And he began to think. "Here am I, sitting watching pigs, hungry and half-starved. Why did I leave my father's comfortable house, where even the lowliest servant gets plenty of bread to eat? I have been foolish and wrong."

He sat there miserably, remembering the old days in his father's home. He remembered the feasts they had had; he remembered the fine clothes, his father's kindness, and the friends who came in to talk. He felt homesick and lonely.

"I shall go back home," he thought, suddenly. "I will go to my father, and I will say to him, 'Father, I have done wrong in God's sight and in yours too, and I am no longer worthy to be called your son. Make me one of your servants, and I will work for you.' "

So he left the pigs and went on his way to his father's house. It was a good distance, and the youth's feet were soon sore with walking on the rough roads.

His father had not forgotten his lost son. Ever since the boy had left, he had been longing to hear from him again and to see him. No letter came, and the old man often wondered where his son was and what he was doing.

Sometimes he climbed up to the flat roof of his house to see if by any chance the youth was coming home. The old man was sure he would know him, even if he were a mile away.

And one day the father saw someone in the distance who reminded him a little of his lost son. It was something in the way he walked, perhaps, or swung his arms.

"But this cannot be my son," thought the father, anxiously. "He is in rags, and he looks poor and miserable. Still it looks like him – yes – it *is* my son!"

Then the father ran down the road to meet the youth. He could not wait to welcome him at the door. He was so glad to see him again. He took him into his arms and kissed him again and again.

The son was overjoyed to be back. "Father," he said, "I have done wrong in God's sight and in yours too, and I am no longer worthy to be called your son."

Before he could say any more, some of the father's servants came running up to see what was happening. The old man turned to them at once.

"Go and find the best suit we have in the house," he said, "and put it on my son. Get a ring to put on his finger, too, as befits a son of mine. Fetch shoes for his feet. Go now and do these things. We will have a great feast to-night, so you must get the calf that we were fattening, and kill it for our supper. We will eat and be merry, for this son of mine I thought was dead is alive again; he was lost, but now he is found."

Then the servants went gladly to do as they were told. They dressed the ragged youth in fine clothes, and they put a shining ring on his finger. They bathed his sore feet and gave him new shoes to wear.

In the kitchen a great feast was being prepared. The fatted calf was roasted, and delicious smells hung on the air. The hungry boy was so glad to be home again and to receive such a welcome that he could hardly keep the tears from his eyes. Everyone seemed so glad to see him back.

All but one person. The elder son had been out working in the fields, and had not seen his brother coming back again. He came home from his work that evening, and was surprised to hear merry sounds, and to see a feast going on.

He called a servant to him. "What do these things mean?" he asked. "Why is there music and dancing and feasting? What has happened?"

And the servant answered joyfully. "Your brother has come home again! Your father has ordered the fatted calf to be roasted, and there's a big feast to welcome your brother back."

Then the elder brother was angry and jealous. Why should his father make such a fuss of a boy who had always been an idler, and who had taken his share of the money and gone away and spent it foolishly and wickedly? It was not fair.

"I shall not go in to the feast," thought the elder brother, and he turned away from the door. But the father came out to him and begged him to join the feast.

"Are you not pleased that your brother has returned to us in safety?" he asked.

"Father," said the elder son, angrily, "all these years I have worked for you and obeyed your orders. I never once did anything wrong. But you did not give *me* a calf or even a kid for a feast, so that I might make merry with my friends. But as soon as your younger son comes home again, who took half your money and wasted it with his foolish companions, you welcome him, kill the fatted calf, and give a great feast!"

"Son," said the father gently, "you have been with me all these years, and you know that all I have is yours. You have nothing to complain of. But it is right that we should welcome your brother, and make merry and be glad that he is home again. We thought him dead, but he is alive; he was lost, but now he is found!"

29: JESUS AND THE STORM

Jesus told some of these stories as he sat in the boat, a little way off the shore. The people loved hearing them, and begged for more and yet more. Then at last Jesus was tired, and wanted to rest.

But if he landed on the shore the people would surround him and follow him, and would not leave him for a moment.

"We will take the boat to the other side of the lake," Jesus said to Peter and the others. "Then, when the people see that we are going, they too will go."

So the little fishing-boat was headed out on the open lake. Jesus was very tired and lay down in the boat. It was pleasant to feel the movement of the little ship over the water, and to hear the plash-plash of little waves against the prow. Jesus rested his head on a cushion and fell asleep.

The disciples let him sleep, for they saw how tired he was. But after a while they grew anxious. Peter pointed out a big black cloud that had suddenly blown up over the hills around. Night was falling, and the wind began to rise.

"I hope we're not going to get one of those sudden storms," said Peter, anxiously. "They come so quickly, and we are far out on the lake."

Sometimes sudden, sharp storms blew down on the lake of Galilee from the hills, and in a trice the waves rose high, and any boat unlucky enough to be on the water then was in great danger.

Even as Peter spoke, the wind began to howl round them in the darkness, and the waves rose high, whipped into foam at the tips. The little boat rocked dangerously to and fro.

Jesus still slept on. Waves splashed over the side of the boat, and it seemed as if it would soon be filled with water. The disciples were very much afraid. "We must wake Jesus," they said. "We shall all be drowned!"

So they awoke him, shaking him, crying in his ear above the sound of the wind and the waves. "Master, Master, we shall be drowned! Save us!"

Jesus awoke, and looked round at the darkness and the white tops of the heaving waves that splashed into the boat. He stood up and spoke to the storm.

"Peace, be still!" he said to the wind and the waves. And at once the wind dropped, and the waves became small, so that there was a great calm on the lake. It was as if the storm had never been.

Then Jesus turned to his astonished disciples. "Why are you so afraid?" he said. "Why don't you trust me more?"

The disciples were filled with wonder, and marvelled at Jesus and his power. "What manner of man is this," they said, "that even the wind and the waves obey him?"

30: JESUS AND THE MADMAN

The morning after that night of storm was calm and lovely. "We will not go back home," said Jesus. "I need to rest and to pray. We will sail right across the lake to the farthest side."

So away went the boat and soon came to a country on the other side of the lake. Here the Gadarenes lived, and nearby the disciples could see a little village called Gerasa.

"We will not go to the village," said Jesus. "We will go up into the lonely hillside. I must be alone for a while."

So they all went up the hillside together. And then suddenly an extraordinary thing happened. A man rushed out of the caves, shouting and shaking his fist at them. He had no clothes on, his hair and beard were long, and altogether he was a terrifying sight.

He was a madman who lived in the caves where the dead were buried. He was fierce and strong and terrible, and everyone was afraid of him. No one could do anything with him. Sometimes he had been caught and had been tied up with ropes and chains, but when he fell into one of his dreadful rages, he was as strong as a giant, and could easily break both ropes and chains.

He often rushed out at people to frighten them, and both men and women fled when he came. They were afraid he might kill them or hurt them. He often hurt himself too, for he would find sharp stones and cut himself with them till he bled.

And now here he was, on this lovely morning, rushing out upon Jesus and his disciples, screaming and shouting, his arms bleeding where he had cut them.

But when the madman saw Jesus he did not hurt him or try to kill him. He fell at his feet and tried to grasp his ankles.

The disciples looked down at him in fear and disgust – but Jesus was neither afraid nor disgusted. He was sorry for this poor wretch whose mind was so crazy and muddled that he could not live as other people did. He looked into the wild, upturned face of the man and spoke gravely to him in the voice that made people listen.

"What is your name?" Jesus said.

"My name!" cried the man. "I have a thousand names, for there are a thousand bad devils inside me, making me do wicked things, and I have as many names as there are devils!"

"Then I will take the thousand devils out of you," said Jesus, speaking quietly, for the man was terribly excited. "They shall all leave you. You shall be yourself again."

The man listened to that quiet voice and looked into those grave, steady eyes, so full of love and understanding and pity. And something happened to him. His madness left him. He became quiet and still. He trembled because he suddenly felt so different and strange. He could think slowly and sensibly. He was no longer mad, but like an ordinary person.

A great gladness and thankfulness welled up in the poor man's heart. He gazed at Jesus with love and gratitude. He looked down at himself, dirty, without clothes, and bleeding. One of the disciples saw that he was ashamed, and he gave the man his cloak.

The madman could not leave Jesus. He sat at his feet, listening to him. He thought that Jesus was the kindest and most wonderful man in the world, and he never wanted to leave him. The poor man had never thought anyone could care enough for him even to give him a kind word.

He was glad, and Jesus was glad, and the disciples were happy to see the good that their master had done. But there was someone on the hillside nearby who was angry.

This was a man who herded a big flock of pigs there. When the madman had come screaming out of the caves and had made such a noise and disturbance, the pigs had taken fright, and had rushed off down the hillside towards the lake. They had not been able to stop themselves, for there were so many of them, and when they came to a steep cliff they fell over one by one and were drowned in the lake.

The man who looked after the pigs was horrified. He had lost hundreds belonging to the people of the village! What would they say? He set off to tell them at once.

"Your pigs are gone!" he called out as he reached the village. "They just seemed to go mad! I can't think what happened to them. And you know that crazy madman who lives in the caves nearby the pigs? Well, he's all right again! He came screaming out of the caves near the pigs, and went to meet some people coming up the hillside. And one of them cured him. He's not mad any more."

"Well, his madness must have gone into our pigs!" said one of the villagers, indignantly. "How dare he do a thing like that? Who cares about the madman? Our pigs are much more valuable. We will not have this stranger in our country, curing madmen and sending the madness into our animals. We will tell him to go!"

So they all went to find Jesus and his disciples, and when they came to the hillside they were astonished to see the man who was once mad sitting down at Jesus' feet, clothed and in his right mind, listening eagerly to all that the Master said.

But the people were too angry about their pigs to pay much attention to the man who had once been mad. They felt certain that Jesus had only cured him by sending away his madness into their pigs – and now they had lost them!

All the same, they felt a little afraid of a man who could do such things. They stood and looked at him, and then became bold enough to go to him.

"Will you please leave our country?" they said. "We don't want you here."

And so Jesus and his disciples got up to go. But the madman caught hold of Jesus in dismay.

"Don't go!" he besought him. "Don't leave me – or at least let me come with you. I never want to leave you again, after what you have done for me."

But Jesus shook his head. "If you want to show me real gratitude, you will stay here," he said. "Go into your own country and tell all that has happened to you. Then if I or my disciples come again, you will have prepared the way for us."

So the man stayed behind and did as Jesus said. He never forgot the man who had come so unexpectedly one fine morning, and had cured him of his terrible madness – and because of his great gratitude he went throughout his country, telling everyone of Jesus.

31: THE LITTLE DAUGHTER OF JAIRUS

"We will sail back home," said Jesus, to his disciples; so they got into the little fishing-boat and set sail once more across the lake.

"Look, Master! There are still crowds of people waiting for you," said Peter, as they came near the shore. "Don't stop to preach to them this morning. Let us have food and rest."

There were hundreds of people waiting for Jesus to come back, all eagerly longing to see him. But among them was a man whose heart was full of trouble, and who was longing for Jesus more than anyone else there.

He was Jairus, a rich man, a ruler of the church. He lived with his wife and little girl in the town. They were very happy together, and the child, who was now twelve years old, was a great companion for her parents.

But now she had fallen ill and was in bed. She was so ill that Jairus, her father, felt certain she was dying. He would lose her, and she was the only child he had. He was full of despair. The doctor could do nothing for her, and the poor parents could only sit by her bedside and watch their child getting worse and worse.

"Can't we ask this healer, Jesus, to come?" he wondered, suddenly. "I believe he is in the town. I will go to find him and beg him to come, and lay his hand on our little daughter. She will surely die if we do not do something for her."

"Go now," said his wife. "Ask where he can be found. He will come, for people say he is goodness itself."

So Jairus went to find Jesus. He asked in which house he was staying, and he went there. But alas! Jesus was not there. "He may be down by the lakeside, preaching," he was told.

So Jairus went down to the lake, and there he saw a crowd of people. Eagerly he pressed through them, seeking Jesus. But he could not find him.

"Jesus has gone across the lake in Peter's boat," said somebody. "He was here last night, telling us stories. Then he and his friends set sail across the lake. We are waiting for them to come back. They may not be long."

But every minute of waiting seemed an hour to Jairus. He thought with despair of his poór little girl, perhaps dying this very minute, and he not with her. But he dared not leave the lakeside in case Jesus came whilst he was gone.

He looked out across the calm blue waters. He would not know which was Peter's boat and which was not. He asked somebody if they knew the boat.

"Yes," answered the man. "I shall know it when it comes. Wait – is that it – coming over there?"

Jairus felt his heart beginning to beat fast – but it sank when the man went on. "No. That's not the boat after all. It's one rather like it."

Then suddenly a cry went up. "There's the boat, look! It's coming! Jesus is coming!"

And there was Peter's boat, coming up with the breeze that blew over the lake. In it stood Jesus, looking out at the waiting people. The boat grounded and the disciples leapt out to pull it in. It was not long before Jesus stood on the shore, whilst his disciples tried to keep the people from surging too closely round their tired Master.

Jairus was not where Jesus landed. He had to press his way through the crowd. "Let me through," he begged. "I must get to him. Let me through!"

The crowd let him pass, and he came to Jesus. He flung himself down at his feet, and began to beg and pray him to come to his little daughter.

"She lies at the point of death," said Jairus. "I pray you, come and lay your hands on her, that she may be healed; then she will live."

The poor man was in such despair that Jesus did not waste a moment, but turned to follow him to his house. All the people who had been listening and watching followed close about him.

"He's going to the house of Jairus," they said eagerly to one another. "He's going to heal his little girl. You know her, don't you? She's ill, poor little thing. We must go and see what Jesus does. He is sure to do something wonderful."

So the crowd jostled about Jesus as he went with Jairus, trying to get as near to him as they could.

Now, in the crowd, there was a woman who had heard of Jesus. She had a disease in her body that she did not want to tell anyone about. She had spent all the money she had on doctors, but instead of getting better she had got worse. She had been ill for twelve years and despaired of ever getting better.

But here, in Capernaum, she had heard of the man called Jesus. She had listened whilst excited people had told of the wonders he had done – how he had healed a palsied man who had been let down through the roof – how he had even healed a leper – and she had wondered if she could see this man too.

She knew she would not dare to speak to him and tell him what was the matter with her. So what would be the good of going to find him?

"But I believe that if I could just *touch* the hem of his robe, or the tassel on his cloak, I should be made better," thought the woman. "He sounds so good and so wonderful. I hardly think I would need to ask him for his help. If I just touched him, without his knowing it, that might be enough to cure me!"

So, whilst Jesus was walking past with Jairus, this woman slipped into the crowd. She had caught sight of Jesus' face, and she knew he could help her. She made her way into the thick of the crowd, getting nearer and nearer to him. Her heart beat as she came just behind him. She put out a trembling hand to touch the bottom of his cloak.

And even as she touched it, she felt herself healed. A change came into her diseased body, and she was better. There was nothing wrong with her at all. The woman was full of wonder and thankfulness. She tried to edge away through the crowd to go back home.

But Jesus stopped and looked round. "Who touched me?" he said.

"*I* didn't," said one.

"Nor did I," said another.

"Master, what do you mean, *who touched you*?" said Peter.

The little girl opened her eyes and sat up . . .

"See the crowd around you, jostling against you, brushing your clothes all the time! Scores of people have touched you."

But Jesus knew that someone had touched him for a purpose, and he had, at that moment, felt goodness going out of him. Someone had wanted his help and his power, and, even without asking for it, that someone had got it. Who was it?

Jesus looked round at all the people near him, his eyes searching their faces. Jairus stood by his side, torn with anxiety, for he so badly wanted Jesus to hurry home with him, before it was too late.

The woman who had touched him felt the eyes of Jesus on her, and she came forward, trembling. She knelt down before him, and, in a low voice, told him of the disease she had had, and of how she had been cured by touching the clothes of Jesus.

"I knew I should be cured," she said. "I knew it. And I am."

Jesus looked at her, glad to find that someone had such faith in him. "Daughter," he said, "because you trusted so much, you were healed. Go in peace, for you will not be ill again."

Now even as he spoke, and Jairus stood impatiently by, waiting, there came messengers through the crowd to find Jairus. The man saw them coming and his heart sank, for he saw by their faces that they brought bad news.

"Sir," said the messengers, who had come from Jairus's own house, "do not trouble Jesus any longer. Your little girl is dead!"

Despair was in the father's heart when he heard this, but Jesus turned to him and spoke: "Don't be afraid. Only believe."

Jesus walked on with Jairus, the large crowd following. At last they got to the house, and Jesus turned round and spoke to the crowd.

"Come no farther!" he said. Then he bade James and Peter and John come with him into the house, and went in with Jairus.

As they went in, they heard a tremendous noise of weeping and wailing and sad singing and chanting. It was the custom in those days to pay people to cry and wail when anyone died, and these people had come to lament for the little girl.

Jesus did not like this noise. He stopped and spoke to the woman. "Why do you make this noise?" he asked. "The little girl is not dead, but asleep."

Then everyone laughed at him, for they knew the child was dead. Jesus put them out of the house, and then he went into the room with the child's mother and father, and his disciples, and stood by the bed where the little girl lay.

Jesus looked down at the little still child. Her eyes were shut and she did not move. The mother cried softly, and the father stood beside her, white and anxious.

Jesus put out his hand and took the child's hand in his. "Little maid," he said, "I say unto you, arise!"

And the little girl opened her eyes and sat up. She got out of bed and walked, astonished that everyone should gaze at her in such amazement. Then her parents took her into their arms and hugged her, hardly daring to believe that she was alive again, smiling and talking to them in her usual way.

"Tell no one of this," said Jesus to Jairus. Then he turned to the mother. "Give your child something to eat," he said, and the mother smiled at him in joy. She had never before been so happy as in the minute in which her darling dead child had come to life.

32: THE BOY WITH THE LOAVES AND THE LITTLE FISHES

So many people came every day to crowd around Jesus and his disciples that sometimes it seemed they had not even time to eat.

"We will go into some deserted place for a while," said Jesus. "Somewhere lonely and far-off, where we shall have peace and rest for a while, and where I can talk to you, for there are still many things you must learn from me before I leave you."

Sometimes Jesus spoke to his disciples of leaving them, and that made them sad. But Jesus knew that he had many enemies, and that one day he would be captured, and might be put to death. He must teach his disciples all he knew before that happened, for, when he left them someone must still carry on the work he had begun.

Jesus had heard that his cousin, John the Baptist, had been killed, and this had made him sad. He was longing to go away from the crowds for a while, and think and pray with only his disciples to keep him company.

"Shall we go to Bethsaida?" asked Peter. He had been born there and knew the country-side well. Part of it was wild and lonely, but very beautiful. There were only small villages around. Jesus would be able to rest in peace for a day or two.

So they all set off in the boat, and sailed over the lake of Galilee till they came to the place Peter knew. It was certainly lovely, and looked as lonely as anyone could wish.

"We will go up into the hills," said Jesus. So they made the boat fast, and then walked up the grassy hillside and sat down where they could get a lovely view of the lake and the distant hills.

But many people had seen Jesus sailing away with his disciples in the boat, and they made up their minds to follow him. They had not got boats of their own, but they could walk round the lake and find out where he was! They could take their ill friends with them, and ask him to make them better.

And so hundreds of people began to hurry round the lake-side, trying to keep the fishing-boat in sight. Where was it going? They would find out, even if it took them all day to get there! Mothers carried their babies, and smaller children ran by their side. Men walked along, and friends carried sick people.

Now when these people began to pour down the roads that led to the country round about Bethsaida, the villagers there were most astonished. The children ran out to ask what the excitement was. Their district was usually so quiet and lonely. What could be bringing all these people here so suddenly?

One small boy reached a little crowd first. "What is the matter?" he asked. "Why are you all coming here? Has anything happened?"

"Jesus is somewhere in your district," answered a woman. "Have you not heard of him? He is a wonderful healer."

"He makes sick people well, and dead people live," said a child, to the boy. "He can do anything. And he tells us the most wonderful stories."

"Come with us and hear him," said a boy, coming up. "There is no telling what he will do. He has the kindest face too, and he likes children near him."

"I wish I *could* come," said the small boy.

"Go and ask your mother," said the other children, and the boy ran off quickly.

"What is the matter, child?" asked his mother, when he ran into the house, where she was at work.

"Mother, there is a wonderful man here to-day, and everyone is going to see him," said the boy. "Can I go too? I've never seen so many people here before. Mother, this man does wonders. Can I go and see him?"

His mother smiled at him. "Yes, you may go," she said. "But wait a little, and let me get some food for you to take. I have a few little loaves you can have, and two pickled fish. Take those with you."

His mother packed up the five little loaves and the two small fishes into a basket. She gave it to the boy, He called good-bye and ran off down the hillside. The crowds of people were still coming along the paths. The boy had never in his life seen so many.

He joined the crowds and they went along until they came to the grassy hillside where Jesus had gone with his disciples. He had already seen the crowds, and knew that he would get no rest that day, as he had hoped.

"They are like sheep without a shepherd," said Jesus, and he went to greet the coming crowds.

Then began a busy day for Jesus and his disciples. The small boy had never seen such marvels in his life. He watched the disciples go among the crowds and seek out sick people to bring to their Master. He went with them and saw Jesus make them well. He listened to him when he sat down and began to tell stories. He peeped behind the grown-ups when Jesus went about to talk to people in the distance, who could not hear what he said.

It was a wonderful day for the lad. For one thing it was exciting to be with so many people after his quiet village life, and for another the boy had never imagined that such wonders could be done for anyone. He carried his basket of food with him wherever he went, but he was so excited and happy that he did not once think of eating.

The day wore on and the evening came. The people still sat there, but they looked hungry and tired. They had walked a long way, and had had nothing to eat.

"Master," said the disciples, coming to Jesus," should we not send the people away, so that they can go into the villages and buy themselves bread?"

"You must give them food to eat," said Jesus.

"It would cost more than two hundred shillings to feed so many people," said Philip, who kept the money belonging to the disciples. "Do you want us to go and buy meat for them?"

"Has no one any food?" asked Jesus. "Go and see!"

So the disciples went round the crowds, asking if anyone had food to share. But the people shook their heads. Those who had brought a little food had already eaten it earlier in the day, but most people had had nothing at all. There seemed to be no food in the whole of that great company.

"Has anyone any bread?" came the voices of the disciples, as they went round. The little boy heard the question. He remembered his basket of food. He unwrapped the cloth into which his mother had put his food, and saw inside the five small loaves and the two little pickled fishes.

He looked at them. Dare he take the food to the disciples?

There was not much in the basket to share with anyone, that was certain. Then the boy heard the question again. "Has anyone any bread?"

The boy pushed through the crowd around him and went up to the nearest disciple. "I have a little bread," he said, "and there are two small fishes as well. Are they any use?"

The disciple took the lad by the hand and led him to Jesus. "Master," he said, "there is a boy here with five loaves and two fishes."

The boy was excited to be taken up to the wonderful man he had watched all day. He stood beside him, looking up with wide eyes. Jesus smiled at him and took the basket.

"This is just what I needed," he said. Then he turned to his disciples.

"Tell the people to sit down in companies of fifty so that we can feed them easily," he said. And the disciples went among the crowds, commanding this. The boy stood by Jesus and watched the people sitting down in fifties, some in rows and some in groups. He wondered what Jesus was going to do.

Then Jesus took the loaves out of the basket and broke them. He looked up to heaven and blessed the bread. Then he gave it to his disciples, and he divided the two fishes as well. One after another the disciples came up to get bread and fish, and Jesus always had his hands full and gave them plenty. He went on breaking the bread and dividing up the fish, and the little boy stood and watched him, more amazed than he had ever been in his life before.

There seemed no end to his bread and fishes! Jesus gave out more and more, and the disciples carried it to company after company of the hungry people. There must have been five thousand there, on the slopes of the green hill, but every one of them was fed.

The small boy had his share too. He sat and ate it, filled with astonishment. "My mother baked the bread and I caught the little fishes," he kept thinking. "And this man Jesus has taken them and made them into enough food to feed all these people. What will Mother say when I tell her? She will not believe me. How proud I am to think that my lunch is feeding all these people. I hope they like Mother's bread."

Jesus and his disciples ate too. The boy spoke shyly to them. "My mother baked this bread, and I caught the fish in the lake."

"I coulu not have done without them," said Jesus, seriously, and his eyes smiled at the boy.

Jesus smiled at him and took the basket . . .

Then, when everyone was fed, and the ground was littered with pieces, Jesus told his disciples to go round and collect the scraps. The hillside must not be spoilt, and nothing must be wasted. The boy helped them, gathering pieces into his own little basket too. And when all the fragments were taken up, there were twelve baskets full of them.

"It is very strange," thought the boy. "I brought only one basketful – and yet we have filled twelve baskets with the scraps."

He was tired when he went home that night, but his heart was glad. He ran into his house to find his mother. She knew something had happened, because his eyes were shining.

"Mother, the bread you baked and the fish I caught fed thousands of people," said the boy. "Listen, and I will tell you! Oh, Mother – this has been the greatest day of my life."

33: ON THE WAY TO JERUSALEM

Although Jesus was loved by thousands of people, and followed by crowds wherever he went, there were many who were jealous of him and hated him. They were important men, learned in the many laws of the church.

They were jealous because the common people flocked to hear Jesus' simple words and stories rather than hear their learned lectures. They were angry because Jesus seemed to break the law in so many little ways.

But they were even more angry with him because he saw through their pretence of being good and noble, and showed clearly that they were selfish and insincere.

Most of these men lived in the big city of Jerusalem, where the Temple of God stood. Jesus was not safe there – but the time came when he felt that he must go to the city and preach the Word of God. Perhaps the people would listen to him – and perhaps, alas! the Pharisees and priests who hated him might also find a chance to capture him and punish him.

Jesus set off on the long way to Jerusalem with his disciples. As always, people thronged around him, begging him, if they were ill, to make them well, asking him questions, calling out for stories. Jesus helped all those in trouble or distress, and preached to all who would listen.

Now as he went, he and his disciples saw many other travellers on the road, going to Jerusalem to join in a festival there. It was difficult to find somewhere to sleep at night, for the villages were crowded with the travellers.

So one night Jesus sent his disciples in front of him to a little village to ask for shelter there. But this village was in Samaria, and the people who lived there, the Samaritans, did not like the folk from Galilee.

"We are on our way to Jerusalem," said the disciples. "Can you give us shelter for the night?"

"No," said a Samaritan, roughly, "we can't."

"We don't want you in our village," said another.

"We don't give shelter to such as you," said a third.

The disciples were angry at this rude reception. They hurried to Jesus to tell him what horrible people the Samaritans were.

"Lord, they say they will not let us sleep in their village!" they said indignantly.

"They cannot know whom they are turning away," said James.

"Master, let us punish them!" cried John. "Shall we call down fire from heaven to burn up all these rude villagers?"

Jesus looked at his angry disciples sadly. Had they learnt so little from him that they should expect him to behave in this way, like a spiteful child?

"That is not the right way to think," he told the angry men. "Surely you know that I have come to save men's lives, not to destroy them! We will walk on to another village."

And so they did. The disciples talked a good deal among themselves about the rude Samaritans in the village, and said how right it was that all Samaritans should be hated. They were bad people, and it was no wonder that everyone despised them, said the disciples.

Jesus was sad to hear this, and to know that everyone thought the same of the Samaritans. It was so stupid to judge a whole people, and label them all bad. Jesus thought about this, and one day he put his thoughts into a wonderful little story, which you shall hear.

It happened that a clever man, very learned in the Law, wanted to test Jesus with questions to see what he would say. He stood up in front of all the listening people, so that everyone could hear what Jesus said to him. After he had asked a question or two, Jesus asked him one also.

"Now, you know everything about the Law of God, and what is written there. Tell me what you think is important in the Law."

The man answered at once. "The Law says that we must love God with all our heart, with all our soul, with all our strength, and with all our mind, and we must love our neighbour as much as we love ourselves."

"You are right," said Jesus. "Do these things, and you shall live with God."

But the man still had another question. "And who is my neighbour?" he asked. "Tell me!"

And then Jesus told him the story of a man who was robbed. Here it is.

34: THE TALE OF THE GOOD SAMARITAN

"Now," said Jesus, "there was once a man who was travelling along the lonely mountainous road that goes from Jerusalem to Jericho. . . ."

As he went along, robbers saw him from their hiding-places among the rocks. They pounced upon the traveller and captured him. They took no notice of his cries. There was no one to hear him, no one to help him.

The robbers took all the man's belongings for themselves. "We will take his clothes too," they said, and they stripped him of each of his garments. Then they hit him again and again, and left him, carrying away the goods they had stolen.

The man was badly hurt. He could not walk. He could only lie on the roadway and groan. His head bled and he was in great pain. If only someone would come by! Then he would get help. He was half-dead. He would surely die before the evening if someone did not help him.

Now along the road came the sound of feet. The wounded man felt hope come into his heart. He tried to lift his head to see who was coming. To his joy he saw a priest. Surely he would help him!

The priest had been to Jerusalem to help in the Temple. As he came along he heard the man groaning and saw him lying bleeding by the roadside.

But the priest crossed over to the other side, and went on his way. He did not even stop to see how badly hurt the wounded man was.

The man could hardly believe it when he saw the priest, the man of God, walking by without helping him. He groaned again and his head fell back. He listened to the priest going down the road.

The Good Samaritan

"Perhaps someone else will come," thought the man. "If only someone comes before it is too late. I shall die in the night!"

Then there came the sound of other footsteps coming along. The man lifted his aching head once more. Yes – here was another traveller, a Levite, a man used to being in the Temple and worshipping God. He would help, he would be kind.

The Levite saw the wounded man by the side of the road. "I suppose he has been set upon by robbers," he thought. "I'll go and have a look at him."

So, to the man's joy, the Levite crossed over the road and bent over him. He saw that the man's clothes had been stripped off. He saw that all his goods had been stolen, for the man had nothing at all. He saw that he had been cruelly beaten, and struck about the head.

And, having seen all this, the Levite turned and went calmly on his way again. He was not going to trouble himself to help the wounded man.

The poor man still lay by the roadside, getting weaker and weaker. He had given up all hope of being helped. Then there came the sound of footsteps once more.

The wounded man lifted his head to see who the traveller was. He saw a man from Samaria, a Samaritan, going that way on business.

"He will not help me," thought the man, sadly. "I have always heard that Samaritans are no good. Why, the priests and the Levites think themselves far better than the Samaritans, and wouldn't even sleep in the same house with one. How unlucky I am!"

The Samaritan was riding a little donkey, and as he came along he was thinking of his business. His eyes were on the road ahead, and he suddenly saw the wounded man lying by the wayside.

"Now what is this?" thought the Samaritan, and he rode right up to the man. He got off his donkey and bent over him. He saw with pity in his heart the bruises and bleeding wounds that the poor man had all over his body.

"Robbers have set upon him," thought the Samaritan, looking all round to make sure there were none nearby. "How they have beaten him! Poor fellow – what can I do for him? I must rub something on these wounds, or they will never heal."

He went to his donkey, and took from his luggage some bottles. In them were oil and wine. The Samaritan emptied a little out, and then gently rubbed the man's wounds with the oil and wine.

Then, having made them clean, he bound them up with strips of cloth.

"Is that better?" he asked. "Can you stand? If you can, I will take you to my donkey and you shall ride him, for you cannot walk. I can hold you on."

The wounded man could hardly stand, but with the Samaritan's help he staggered to the little donkey, and his kind friend helped him on. Then, holding him steady, the Samaritan guided the donkey along the road.

It was wonderful to feel his aching wounds soothed, but even more wonderful to know there was someone so kind and pitiful that he could do all this for a wounded man. But the Samaritan had not yet finished with him. Walking beside the donkey all the way, he took the man to a roadside inn, and called the inn-keeper.

"I must have a good room for this poor fellow," he said. "He has been robbed, and is very much hurt. "I will look after him to-night and try to make him better. Give me a good room for him."

The wounded man was soon comfortably in bed. The Samaritan bathed his wounds again, and gave him food and drink. "Now sleep," he said. "In the morning you will feel better."

The man slept. He awoke in the morning, weak and aching, but much better. The Samaritan saw that he would live, if he were taken care of. So he went to the inn-keeper.

"I have to go now," he said. "But I want you to look after this man for me. Look, here is some money! You can spend this on him, and give him what he wants till he is well again, and able to leave."

"I will do that, sir," answered the inn-keeper, and he took the money.

"If you should spend more money than I have given you, tell me when I come again, and I will give you more," said the Samaritan, and went on his way, riding his little donkey.

When Jesus had finished telling this story, he looked at the learned man who had asked him how he could know which was his neighbour.

"Now," said Jesus, looking at the listening man, "which of the three travellers – the priest, the Levite, or the Samaritan – was a good neighbour to the man that fell among thieves?"

And the man answered. "He that showed kindness to him."

"You are right," said Jesus. "Now go and do the same – show kindness to all who need it, and love your neighbour as much as you love yourself!"

35: JESUS AND THE LITTLE TAX-COLLECTOR

Jesus and his disciples came to Jericho, on their way to Jerusalem. As usual, there were crowds to welcome him, for everyone in the city wanted to see him.

Now there was in Jericho a very rich man who was much hated by the people. This was a tax-collector called Zacchaeus. All the tax-gatherers were disliked, because they were usually dishonest and charged people more than they should. They put a great deal of the money into their own pockets, and so they became very rich indeed.

Zacchaeus was very wealthy, and he had a fine house and servants. But the people of Jericho would not have anything to do with him. "He is a wicked little man!" they said. "He robs us, when we have to pay our taxes. We will not know him, or go to his house."

Now at times Zacchaeus felt ashamed of himself and his riches, for he knew that he had taken them from the people unfairly. This did not always worry him, but it did sometimes, especially when people he would have liked to have for friends turned their backs on him. He was not altogether a hard and wicked man, as many tax-collectors were, but he had some good in him, struggling to come out.

One day Zacchaeus heard that Jesus was coming to Jericho. He was on the way! Like everyone else the tax-gatherer had heard of the things that Jesus said, and the many wonderful things he had done. Probably Zacchaeus knew too that Jesus had actually chosen two tax-collectors as disciples. Zacchaeus felt that he really must see him.

So when he saw the crowds forming in the street, Zacchaeus went to join them. He was a little man, and he soon realised that he would have no chance at all of seeing Jesus unless he got well to the front. He could not possibly see over everyone's shoulders.

The crowd would not let him get to the front even though he was so short. They all knew Zacchaeus, the hated tax-collector! So they pushed him back whenever he tried to squeeze through, and they called him rude names.

Zacchaeus was almost in despair. At this rate he wouldn't get even a glimpse of the wonderful preacher. Then an idea came to him. He would climb a tree! He knew the very one to climb, a great big one, whose branches spread right over the roadway. If he climbed out on to a spreading branch he could easily see Jesus coming along.

"I'll climb up now," said Zacchaeus to himself. "I can hear shouts from far down the road. That must mean that Jesus is coming."

He ran to the big tree. He climbed up it quickly on his short legs. Then he slid out on to the broad branch that overhung the roadway.

Far down the road Jesus walked, the people crowding round him. As he came near it was easy for Zacchaeus to pick him out, for there was something so noble in his face, and in his steady eyes, that even a child could tell at once that here was someone both good and great.

Zacchaeus peered down through the leaves, feasting his eyes on the goodness he saw in Jesus' face. Jesus came nearer and nearer. And then Zacchaeus had the greatest surprise of his life!

Just as he reached the tree, Jesus looked up. He saw little Zacchaeus looking down at him intently, and, as he always did, Jesus read what was in his heart. He saw there a real longing for goodness, and he knew that Zacchaeus was not altogether bad, although he was a hated tax-collector, often dishonest in his dealings with the people.

Now Jesus never lost a chance of bringing out any goodness or kindness that lay in anyone's heart. It was his work to help the foolish, the weak and the wicked. So he spoke at once to the little tax-collector in the tree. He even knew the man's name!

"Zacchaeus!" he said. "Make haste and come down, because to-day I want to come to your house."

It was a wonder that Zacchaeus did not fall out of the tree with astonishment and delight. To think that this wonderful man, with the noble face, should call out to him, Zacchaeus, the hated collector, and say that he was coming to his house! What an honour! What a marvellous surprise!

Zacchaeus slid down the tree at once. The people stared at him silently. They were not pleased to see smiles on the face of this little man they hated so much. They were surprised at Jesus. Why should he choose to go with a man like Zacchaeus? Ah, the stories they could tell of that dishonest fellow!

Zacchaeus rushed off to his house to prepare a welcome for Jesus. His heart was singing for joy. He felt that Jesus was the most wonderful, the most understanding person he had ever met in his life. What did it matter if everyone else turned his back on him, if only Jesus would come into his house?

Jesus went to the tax-collector's house and sat down with his disciples to eat the feast that Zacchaeus had had prepared for him. The little man could not do enough for him, for he felt so happy and so grateful.

But outside the door the crowds murmured against Zacchaeus. They could see Jesus inside, eating with the man they hated. They were jealous of Zacchaeus. He should not have the honour of having Jesus in his house! He was a wicked fellow.

"Such an honour will only make Zacchaeus worse!" they said to one another. "He will think himself Somebody, and will rob us more than ever when he takes our taxes. He is a bad man."

Zacchaeus could hear what the people said, because they spoke loudly, meaning to hurt him. He knew perfectly well that he could expect them to say bad things, for he deserved them. He was too proud and happy even to feel angry – but he was ashamed to think that Jesus should hear them.

He looked at his guest, and Jesus looked back at him, steadily and kindly. All the hidden good that lay in the heart of Zacchaeus flowered at once, and he knew what he must do. He must show this great man that he, Zacchaeus, was able to do right, in spite of what everyone said.

So Zacchaeus stood up and spoke loudly to Jesus, so loudly that the listening people by the door could hear what he said, and could pass it on to the others.

"Behold, Master!" said Zacchaeus. "I am going to give half of my goods to the poor. And if I have ever taken any money wrongly from a man, then I will give it back to him four times over!"

And then, looking at the happy face of their Master, all the disciples knew that once again he had been right, and had found the hidden goodness that lay deep down in the heart of the dishonest little tax-collector. He had chosen to stay in the house of a sinner – and because of this, he had changed the whole life of a man who was hated and despised.

"You are one of God's children," said Jesus to Zacchaeus, and the little tax-collector looked back at him with shining eyes. That was the happiest day of his life.

36: HAPPINESS FOR A BLIND MAN

Jericho was a big city, and many people passed in and out. The beggars sometimes got a few pence from the passers-by, and they sat by the roadside, watching the travellers, begging for a few coins.

Among the beggars was a blind man called Bartimaeus. He could not see the passers-by, but he could hear their footsteps. He called out for their pity, and sometimes they dropped a penny into his outstretched hand. He was a poor wretch, unable to work because of his blindness. All he could do was to sit by the wayside each day, hoping for a little charity from someone with a kind heart.

One day, as he sat there in the sunshine, his sharp ears heard the sound of more footsteps hurrying by than was usual. It sounded to Bartimaeus as if there were scores of people on the road! He listened hard and then it seemed as if there were even more going by – hundreds! What could be the matter?

"What is all the excitement about?" shouted Bartimaeus at last. "Won't somebody tell me? I can't see for myself."

"It's Jesus of Nazareth!" somebody answered. "He's coming by here. We're going to watch for him. He's coming quite soon."

"Jesus of Nazareth!" said Bartimaeus to himself. "Why, that's the great healer. Coming by here! If only he would see me! It's too good to be true. Jesus of Nazareth! Oh, what can I do to make him see me?"

The crowds grew thicker and more excited. Jesus was near. He came walking down the wide road, talking to the men and women near him. Bartimaeus felt certain that Jesus was nearby now. If only he could know for certain – but he was blind, and could see nobody.

Then Bartimaeus lifted up his voice and began to shout. How he shouted!

"Jesus, have pity on me! Jesus, have pity on me!"

"Be quiet!" said the people nearby. "How dare you make such a noise!"

Bartimaeus took no notice at all. He went on and on shouting, as loudly as ever he could:

"JESUS! JESUS, HAVE PITY ON ME!"

His voice rose right above the sounds of the crowd, and some of them were angry to think that a beggar should make such a disturbance. They scolded him well, and ordered him to be quiet.

But nothing would quiet Bartimaeus that day. He went on shouting, knowing that that was the only way he had of making Jesus heed him.

"JESUS! HAVE PITY ON ME!"

Jesus heard the voice shouting so urgently. He stopped and looked all round through the crowds of people. He saw the blind man sitting shouting by the wayside.

"Bring him here to me!" he commanded. Then the people guessed that he was going to heal the blind man and they were glad. They ran to Bartimaeus and spoke to him.

"Get up, fellow!" they said. "Jesus has sent for you!"

Bartimaeus felt his heart beat fast with joy. He got up straight away, and flung his cloak to the ground. He stretched out his hands to feel the way to Jesus, for he could not see anything but darkness. Willing hands took his and guided him to where Jesus stood in the middle of the road.

Jesus looked at blind Bartimaeus with pity. "What do you want of me?" he asked. "Tell me!"

"Lord, if only I could see!" said the beggar.

Jesus put out his hand and touched the man's poor blind eyes – and at once he could see!

Bartimaeus gazed round in wonder and joy. He was no longer in darkness. He was in light and sunshine. He could see the beautiful colours all around. He could see the kind face of the man who had healed him.

And such a great gladness came into his heart that he could not help shouting and singing for joy. He joined the crowd of people following Jesus, who were all marvelling at the healing of the blind man, rejoicing with all their hearts. But the most joyful among them was the beggar Bartimaeus.

37: JESUS AND THE CHILDREN

Jesus always loved little children, and they loved him. They knew he would welcome them, wherever he was, and they loved the stories he told them.

One day, when Jesus was talking to the people, some mothers and fathers, who had small children, thought they would take them to Jesus for him to bless them and put his wonderful hands on them.

So they gathered together their little ones, some being carried in their arms, and others toddling at their sides, and they went to find Jesus.

The disciples saw them coming with the children. One of the mothers spoke to them eagerly. "We have brought our children to Jesus. It will make such a difference to them if he would just bless them. It would help them to grow up good and kind. He is such a wonderful man."

"He's busy," said a disciple, rather unkindly. "He can't see you just now."

"He is talking to many people," said another disciple. "He can't be bothered with children just now. Go away and come back later."

The parents were disappointed. They turned to go away. But Jesus saw their faces, and he called to his disciples:

"Bring the little children to me! Don't stop them coming. They belong to my kingdom just as you do – and, indeed, unless you have the open heart of a little child, you will not be able to enter my kingdom!"

So the mothers and fathers gladly brought their children to him, and he took them into his arms one by one. He blessed them and loved them, and then let them go.

38: THE RICH YOUNG MAN

After Jesus had blessed the little children, he left to go on his way again. Then there came someone running to him. It was a young man, richly dressed, who knelt down in the road before Jesus. He had not come to be healed, but to ask him a question.

"What must I do, Master, to live a noble life?" he asked.

He looked up at Jesus, eager for his answer, for he was a young man really anxious to lead a good and great life. Surely Jesus would tell him what he ought to do!

"You know the Commandments of God," said Jesus. "You have been taught all the things you must do."

"I have kept all the Commandments," said the rich young man. "I have always tried to do what is right – and yet I feel I have not done enough. Is there anything else I can do?"

Jesus looked down into the eager young face, and he loved what he saw there. Here was a really good young man, one to be trusted and loved, one who could be depended upon.

But there was one thing that kept the young man back from doing really great things – and that was his money, for he was very rich.

"There is only one thing wrong with you," said Jesus. "You have too much money, and it is hindering you. Go and sell all you have, give it to the poor, and then come and follow me!"

The young man looked down. He had much money and great possessions. How could he give them all up, and follow Jesus? He turned sorrowfully away and left the little company.

Jesus watched him go, and his face was sad. The young man would have made a wonderful disciple, perhaps one of the best of all.

"How hard it is for a rich man to enter into the Kingdom of God!" said Jesus, sadly.

This astonished the disciples, who thought that everything must be easier for rich people than for poor. But Jesus shook his head.

"You know the little gate called 'Needle's Eye'," he said, "the one we use when we are on foot and want to pass through the walls of the city? Well, I say to you that it is easier for a camel to pass through that tiny gate than for a rich man to enter into the kingdom of God!"

"A camel could never get through that small gate," said the disciples. "Do you mean that rich people can seldom share the kingdom of God? Well, Master, if that is so, poor people surely cannot do better than rich people. Can they too not enter the kingdom?"

"All things are possible with God," said Jesus, and he smiled at the puzzled men.

Jesus himself had no home and no possessions. "The foxes have holes and the birds of the air have their nests," he said, "but I have no home of my own."

He did not want his disciples to think that money and possessions mattered at all. It was the things of the heart that mattered – kindness and justice, love and charity. If a man had these, then he was truly rich, and the kingdom of God was his.

He once told them a story of a prosperous man. He had such wonderful harvests that his barns were filled to overflowing, and the man was proud and pleased.

"I shall pull down my barns and build much bigger ones," he said. "I shall be so rich that I shall be able to take my ease, and eat, drink and be merry for years!"

But that night the man died, and his spirit went to God. He

could not take with him his great possessions. They did not matter at all to God. All that mattered to Him were the things the man brought with him in his heart, the good or the evil, the pure or the impure.

Always Jesus tried to teach his disciples to see clearly the things in life that were worth while, so that they too might preach these things to the people. And then, too, he began to warn them of dreadful things that might happen to him, and to them too.

"We are going to Jerusalem, where I have many enemies," he said. "I warn you that I shall be taken captive, and beaten and mocked, and even put to death."

But the disciples could not understand such things. They could not believe that what Jesus said would be true. Was he not the Son of God, able to perform many miracles? Surely one day he would be a great King, and they would rule with him!

39: JESUS ENTERS JERUSALEM

The roads to Jerusalem were now full of thousands of people who wanted to keep the great spring Festival in the city. Jesus and his disciples saw the great crowds pouring along the way, as they travelled on the rough mountain road.

And now it was time for Jesus to let the people of Jerusalem know that he came to them as God's own son, the Saviour, who could deliver them from all evil, if only they would believe him.

So, when he and his disciples came near a little village called Bethphage, not far from the Mount of Olives, from which Jerusalem could be seen on its own hill, Jesus stopped, and gave an order to two of his disciples.

"Go to the nearby village," said Jesus. "Just where you enter it, you will see a young donkey tied up, one that no one has ever ridden on before. Untie it, and bring it here to me. If anyone says to you, 'Why do you loose the donkey?' answer him in this way – 'Because the Lord has need of him.'"

So two of the disciples set off to the little village. Just as they entered it, they saw a young donkey tied up, and near it was its mother. The disciples began to untie the donkey.

Some men nearby, the owners of the two animals, called out in surprise.

"What do you mean by untying that donkey?"

"The Lord has need of him," answered the disciples. Then the men let the disciples take the donkey. The little thing's mother followed it down the hill, and soon the two donkeys and the disciples joined the others.

Now in those days only soldiers rode on horseback. Men of peace rode on donkeys, and Jesus was a man of peace. All he wanted was to bring peace and happiness to others. He wanted to enter the city of Jerusalem on a mission of peace and love, and so he rode on a donkey.

The disciples were glad to think that their beloved master was going to ride, instead of walk. They took off their cloaks and made a saddle for him to sit on, and some put their cloaks on the roadway for him to ride over. He should be a King!

The little donkey set off, with Jesus on his back. The disciples began to sing and shout loudly.

"Blessed is the King that comes in the name of the Lord! Peace in heaven, and glory in the highest!"

The crowds along the road began to stare. Some were from Galilee, and they knew Jesus and had seen the wonders that he did. Many loved him because he had helped their friends. So they also began to shout and sing.

Some of them took off their cloaks, too, and spread them in the road. When Jesus had passed over them they snatched up their cloaks and spread them again, further down the hillside, for now Jesus was riding down the Mount of Olives, and could see Jerusalem in the distance.

"It's Jesus!" the word went, from mouth to mouth. "It's Jesus! He's riding into Jerusalem like a King! Maybe wonderful things will happen now. Let us welcome him and praise him!"

So the crowds began to shout more loudly than ever! "Hosanna to the Son of David! Blessed is he that comes in the name of the Lord! Hosanna! Hosanna!"

Everyone cheered in this way, and became very excited. Many people stripped the branches off the nearby trees and laid them in the roadway for the donkey to pass over. It was an amazing sight.

The people in Jerusalem heard the shouting and the cheering, and they came out to see what the excitement was.

"It's Jesus of Nazareth!" cried someone. "He's coming into Jerusalem. We must welcome him!"

So the people in Jerusalem itself came to welcome Jesus. When they wanted to be very joyful at any festival, they used to get palm branches from the trees and wave them in the air. And now they took big branches of plumy palm and waved them wildly as they welcomed Jesus.

"Hosanna! Blessed be the King of Israel! . . ."

"Hosanna! Blessed by the King of Israel! Hosanna!"

There were many enemies of Jesus in that great city, and it was not long before the Pharisees and the Chief Priests heard the noise of shouting, and found out what it was.

"It is Jesus again!" they said, angrily. "He has come into our city, and the people are cheering him as if he were a great king! We cannot have this. We will ask him to stop the people from making such a noise." They did not dare to try and capture Jesus, with all the people welcoming him so gladly.

So some of the Pharisees went into the crowd and called out to Jesus:

"Tell your disciples to be quiet!"

Jesus turned to look at them and answered: "If these men should keep quiet on such a day as this, the very stones on the wayside would cry out!"

And thus Jesus entered Jerusalem, riding on the donkey, the people crowding round him happily, giving him a wonderful welcome. But the Pharisees and the Chief Priests were angry and troubled. They could do nothing! They dared not touch this man whom the whole city welcomed!

"It is extraordinary," they said to one another. "We cannot seem to do anything against this man. The whole world has gone after him!"

40: JESUS GOES TO THE TEMPLE

Now a day or two after Jesus had entered Jerusalem, he went to the Temple to pray, and in the beautiful outer courts he found something that filled him with anger and disgust.

The courts were nothing but a market! People bought and sold things there, money was changed, animals were fastened there, and the whole place was noisy and dirty.

Jesus stood and looked at it. He saw the men selling oxen, sheep, goats and doves. He watched the money-changers, changing the Roman money into the coins that the people used for paying their temple-taxes, and he saw that often the money-changers cheated the people. He saw people using the outer courts as a kind of short cut, not caring at all that they were part of the Temple.

The oxen lowed, the sheep bleated, and the money-changers shouted loudly. People called to one another, and went to look at the cages of doves on the stalls. No one would ever have guessed that these courts belonged to a great Temple – the House of God.

Jesus stood looking at the dirty, noisy place, and he could bear it no longer. He shouted to the men there to go! He went to the tables of the money-changers and overturned them, so that their money rolled all over the place! He upset the stalls, and he drove out those who were using the courts as a short cut. He even drove away those who had come to buy, and soon there was a great commotion of people shouting and calling out in anger and amazement.

The passers-by came running it to see what was happening. When they saw Jesus driving everyone away, and upsetting all the tables and stalls, they were amazed.

"What is happening?" they cried. And the money-changers, trying to pick up their money, shouted fiercely to Jesus. "Why do you do this?"

And Jesus answered them sternly. "Do you not know what is written in the Bible?" he said. "It is said there that God's House shall be a House of Prayer! But you have made it a den of thieves!"

Jesus was quite without fear, and no one dared to touch him, not even the angry money-changers. But these men soon complained to the Chief Priests, who sold them the right to trade in the courts. The people themselves delighted to see a man completely fearless, and they came round him at once to hear him preach in the courts of the Temple.

Even the children came to him and cheered him, shouting, "Hosanna to the Son of David." This made the Chief Priests even more angry, but they could do nothing, for the people really loved to hear Jesus preach to them.

Each day Jesus sat in the Temple courts and healed the sick, and talked to the people who came to listen. There was so little time left now, he knew. Soon his enemies would catch him, and that would be the end of his wonderful work, the work he loved so much.

At night Jesus and his disciples went out of the City to the hillsides under the stars. There they slept in safety. The Pharisees and the Priests had their spies everywhere, and were waiting their chance to take Jesus away. There were so few days left in which to work, so few days in which to preach and to heal the sick.

41: THE WIDOW'S GIFT

Jesus sat every day preaching in the Temple. Not only his disciples and friends listened to him, but the Pharisees, the Scribes and the Priests, all of whom were his enemies. They came to listen and to watch, because they were trying to find something in his deeds or words for which they could put him into prison.

Jesus knew this. He saw that they were proud and selfish, insincere and uncharitable, and he warned the people not to be like the Scribes and the Pharisees.

"Although they tell you the Law of God and say what you must and must not do, you must not be like these men," he said to the people. "They only pretend to be good! They make a great show of their goodness, but how they love to get the best places at the feasts, and the highest seats in church! How they love to be bowed down to and called 'Master'. Do not be like them."

The Scribes and the Pharisees were standing nearby when Jesus said this, and it made them very angry. If only they could kill this man!

Then Jesus went to sit quietly in another court. He watched the people going in and out, and his disciples sat and watched them too. It was a busy sight. It was the Festival Week, and thousands of people had come to visit Jerusalem and pray in the Temple.

In this court were set the money-boxes into which people could put money for the Temple and its many charities. There were a good many of these boxes or chests, with a trumpet-like opening into which money could be slipped. Then it fell down into the box.

The people could put as much money as they liked into the boxes, but they had to put in at least as much as a mite. We haven't a coin worth as little as that but in those days there were mites and even half-mites.

Jesus sat watching the people putting in their money. He saw rich men come and put in much money carelessly. They would not miss it! He saw other people putting in what money they could spare.

And then he caught sight of a poor widow woman, whose clothes showed Jesus that she could have very little money indeed! She had no husband to work for her, so she had a hard life.

"Surely," thought Jesus, "this poor woman cannot spare any

of her tiny bit of money to put into the boxes! She cannot have enough to feed herself."

But even as he watched, the woman went up to one of the boxes. Hoping that nobody would notice how little money she was putting in, she slipped two mites, into the box and then hurried away.

Jesus spoke to his disciples. "Did you see that poor widow?" he said. "The rich men have put in plenty of money, but that woman only put in two mites. And yet she put in more than anyone else! They put in what they had to spare – but she put in everything she had. In the eyes of God her small gift is worth more than those of all the rich men together!"

42: JESUS WARNS THE PEOPLE

And now, indeed, the time was drawing near when Jesus would no longer be able to carry on his work. He was sad because his many enemies were blinded by their hate, and would not listen to or understand what he had come to tell everyone.

Jesus knew that hatred and unkindness led to battle and strife and death. He knew that only by listening to his words of love and peace would the people of Jerusalem be saved from terrible things.

One evening his disciples pointed out the enormous stones of which the Temple was built, and marvelled at them. Some of them were so big that they seemed as large as the little white houses dotted about on the hillsides.

Jesus looked at the great stones, and said a surprising thing. "Soon," he said, "not one of these stones shall be left on another! They shall all be thrown down."

"Master, when shall these things be?" said the disciples, in surprise and fear.

And then Jesus began to tell them all that a terrible time was near, a time when hatred and bitterness would bring war to Jerusalem, and to many nations.

"There will be wars and talk of wars," said Jesus, "and one nation will fight against another. There will be earthquakes and famines and terrible diseases. You, my disciples, will have to suffer much for me, for you will be beaten and dragged before rulers and kings, and cast into prison. But do not be afraid, for you will then have your chance to tell everyone about me, and the right words will be put into your mouths.

It will be a terrible time, for parents will turn against their children, and children will betray their parents, and brothers, friends and relations will betray each other. Some of you will be put to death. You will know that these things are near when you see soldiers on the hills around Jerusalem. Then you must flee to the country at once, without stopping to take a single thing with you. You must pray that it will not be winter when these fearful things happen, for if it were they would be all the more terrible.

Jerusalem will be utterly destroyed, and there will be horror and darkness in the land. But one day my kingdom shall come, and my friends will be chosen and brought together. Watch, therefore, for the Master of the House to come, and be ready."

Then Jesus told the story of the ten bridesmaids, so that his disciples might see clearly what he meant when he said that they must always be ready.

43: THE STORY OF THE TEN BRIDESMAIDS

There were once ten bridesmaids who had been invited to join in the wedding procession of the bride and bridegroom. The wedding was to take place at night, for in those days marriages in Israel were always held at night. The ten bridesmaids were told to make ready to join the procession with their lanterns.

"It is impossible to tell you exactly the time when the bridegroom will come," the girls were told. "But you will be warned in good time. So keep your lanterns alight and be ready."

Now the lamps were filled with oil. The ten bridesmaids filled them themselves, and then lighted them, so that they were ready for the procession.

Now five of the girls were wise and five were foolish. The five wise ones were afraid that perhaps their lamps would have burnt all their oil before the wedding procession came along, and then they would not be able to welcome the bridegroom because their lamps would be out. So the wise ones bought themselves extra oil, and kept it beside them, in case they needed it. The five foolish ones only had the oil in their lanterns.

The ten girls went to sleep, their lamps burning beside them. They knew they would be awakened when the wedding procession came along. Then they would jump up, arrange their dresses, take their bright lanterns, and welcome the bridegroom, joining the happy procession at the right moment.

Now the procession was delayed, and it was not until midnight that the bridegroom came along with all his friends. Then there came a cry.

"Behold, the bridegroom comes! Go out to meeet him!"

The ten girls jumped up hastily. They took up their lamps to trim them and make them burn brightly. But the lamps of the five foolish ones had gone out, because the oil was all burnt. So they ran to the five wise ones, who were refilling their lanterns with the oil they had been careful enough to bring with them.

"Give us some of your oil!" cried the five foolish bridesmaids. "Our lamps have gone out."

"We can't," said the wise ones. "We have only enough for our own lamps. You had better hurry to buy oil from some shop."

So the five foolish ones hurrred off to buy more oil for their lamps. And whilst they were gone the bridegroom came, with the wedding procession. Then the five wise bridesmaids joined the procession with their bright lamps, and went on their way to the marriage. They entered into the house and the door was shut.

Soon the five foolish ones came hurring back, their lanterns filled with oil again, and shining brightly. But they found the door shut.

They knocked loudly on it, crying, "Lord, Lord, open the door!"

But a voice came from inside, saying, "I don't know you!" And thus the five foolish bridesmaids missed the feast and stood outside weeping in the darkness.

"And so," said Jesus, "always be ready, for you never know when the Kingdom of Heaven will come."

What Jesus said about the horror of war coming to Jerusalem was true, for many years afterwards the Romans sent hordes of soldiers to crush a big Jewish rebellion. Then, as Jesus had said, soldiers appeared on the hills and Jerusalem was besieged. The people were terrified, and hundreds died by the sword or from starvation.

The City of Jerusalem was taken, and the flames soon burnt it to the ground. The beautiful Temple was knocked down, so that, as Jesus said, not one of its enormous stones was left standing on another. The Jews then had no country of their own, and since that day they have had to live where they could, in other people's lands.

Jesus had not come to bring the Jews an earthly kingdom, or to make them fight against the Romans. He had come to bring a kingdom of love and peace in their hearts and in the hearts of anyone in the world who would listen and understand. It was not the Romans that Jesus wanted his people to fight, but the powers of evil. But it was hard for even his disciples to understand this.

44: THE LAST STORY THAT JESUS TOLD

This story, the last one that Jesus told, is perhaps the most beautiful, and is certainly one of the most important.

"When I come as a great King," said Jesus, "and all the holy angels with me, I shall sit upon my throne. And before me shall be brought all the people who have lived in the world.

"I shall separate them one from another, just as a shepherd separates his sheep from the goats. The good sheep shall be on my right hand, and the goats on my left.

"Then I shall say to those on my right hand, 'Come, blessed children of God's, come into the kingdom that has been prepared for you since the beginning of the world. For when I was hungry you gave me meat, and when I was thirsty you gave me drink. When I was a stranger, you took me in, and when I was in rags, you clothed me. When I was ill you visited me, and when I was in prison, you came to me.'

"Then my good sheep, the happy people on my right hand, shall say to me in surprise: 'But Lord, when did we see you hungry, and give you food? When did we see you thirsty and give you drink? When did we see you a stranger, and take you in, or in rags and clothed you? When did we see you ill or in prison and visited you?'

"And I shall answer and tell them: 'Whenever you did these things to anyone in trouble, even to the very least of my brothers, then you did them to *me*!'

"Then I shall turn to the wicked ones on my left hand, and I shall bid them go away from me into pain and sorrow. 'Depart from me!' I shall say. 'For when I was hungry you gave me no meat, and when I was thirsty you gave me no drink. When I was a stranger you did not take me in, and when I was in rags you gave me no clothes. When I was sick and in prison, you did not visit me!'

"And then those on my left hand shall question me in surprise:

'But Lord, when did we see you hungry or thirsty, a stranger or in rags, ill or in prison?'

"And I shall answer them and tell them: 'Because you did not do these things to those who needed them, you did not do them to *me*!'

"So the good shall take their rightful happiness, but the wicked shall know only sadness and pain."

45: JUDAS, THE TRAITOR

Now, among the disciples was one called Judas. He was a clever man, good at keeping account of what money the disciples had, and good at bargaining for what food the little company needed.

But Judas was not honest. He was not to be trusted. He did not love Jesus as the others did; he loved himself first and foremost.

He followed Jesus because he really believed that Jesus was going to be a great and powerful King. "Then," thought Judas, "I shall be powerful, too. Maybe I shall look after the money that flows into the King's treasury. I shall be very powerful indeed."

But, as the weeks went on, Judas found that the kingdom of which Jesus so often spoke was not the kind that he, Judas, wanted. Judas had no use for a kingdom of love. He wanted a real kingdom, with real money and real power. He began to despise Jesus for not making himself a great King.

"He can do marvellous miracles for other people," thought Judas. "Why then does he not do them for himself and for us? We have given up everything and followed him – surely he ought to reward us by making himself king and giving us power to help him to rule! I would not have followed him if I had not thought this would happen."

When Judas saw that the Chief Priests, the Pharisees and the Scribes were getting angry with Jesus, he was afraid. "We shall all go to prison!" he said. "And that will be the end of any wonderful kingdom!"

He thought over the matter. "I should be foolish if I did not look after myself," he thought. "I shall not stay and be punished if Jesus is captured. I shall go to the Chief Priests and the Rulers of Jerusalem, and I shall tell them I will help them, if they like to pay me. If I help them to capture Jesus, they will reward me well, and I shall be safe."

Now at that time the High Priest of Jerusalem was a man

called Caiaphas. He had been made High Priest some years before by the Romans, who ruled over the land of Israel. He did not want to displease the Romans in any way, for he wanted to be High Priest for as long a time as he could.

He was afraid of Jesus, because he saw that the people loved him, and followed him by the thousand. "Suppose this man should raise an army, and march against the Romans!" thought Caiaphas. "Some of the people say he is their Deliverer, and comes to bring a kingdom of his own. Perhaps that is what he means to do – fight the Romans and make himself King of the Jews. The Romans will crush us again, and I shall be sent to prison because I allowed this man Jesus to begin a rebellion."

So Caiaphas called a meeting of the rulers of Jerusalem. They meant to discuss what they could do to take Jesus and cast him into prison.

"We dare not do anything to him now, whilst the Festival is being held in the City," said Caiaphas. "The town is full of Galileans, and many of them love him. It may cause an uproar among the people if we catch him now. We must wait until this Festival Week is over."

Now just as the rulers had decided this, someone entered their secret meeting. It was Judas the traitor.

The rulers were astonished to see him. Was he not a disciple of the very man they had been talking about?

"What do you want?" asked Caiaphas.

"What will you give me if I help you to catch Jesus?" asked Judas.

The rulers were delighted at this. If only one of his disciples would betray him to them at the right moment, everything would be easy. So Caiaphas spoke eagerly to Judas.

"We will pay you a good deal of money," he said. "We can see you will keep your word to us. You shall be well rewarded, you may be sure."

"Pay me the money now," said Judas who, because he was not trustworthy himself, rarely trusted other people. "How much will you give me?"

"We will give you the price of a slave!" said Caiaphas. "That is thirty pieces of silver – a very good reward. We will give the money to you now."

So they gave thirty pieces of silver to the traitor, and he took them. "I will send you word where you can most easily take Jesus, without the crowd interfering," promised Judas, and left the meeting, carrying the silver.

He went to join Jesus and the other disciples. He held a terrible secret in his heart. He thought that no one of the little company guessed it – but Jesus knew it and was bitterly grieved.

And from that time Judas watched for the moment to come when he might send word to Caiaphas to come and take Jesus. He had sold his Master and his own honour, too, for thirty pieces of silver.

46: THE TIME DRAWS NEAR

The time was drawing near for the enemies of Jesus to come upon him. It seems strange to us that there should have been so many people who wanted to harm and kill a man who spent his days in healing the sick, and preaching love and kindness to all who would listen.

The leaders of the people were jealous of Jesus' growing power. They hated him because he saw through their pretence of being good, and told the people not to be like them. It was so much easier to *pretend* to be good than it was to *be* good! But how the rulers hated to have their pretence shown up for what it was!

Jesus had other enemies too. There were the goody-goody people who thought that Jesus was foolish to make friends with such people as Zacchaeus the tax-collector, and other men and women who had a bad name. Why should he prefer those who were sinners? They could not understand that Jesus specially wanted to help the sinners, and they were angry with him because he seemed to prefer them.

Then there were the traders whose tables of money Jesus had overturned in the outer courts of the Temple, and the men whose animals he had driven out on the same day. They hated him, too, and spoke against him whenever they could.

Others, who had followed him at first, deserted him because, like Judas, they were disappointed. They had hoped he was going to be a great King and Deliverer, and that he would lead them against the hated Romans, and use his miraculous powers to make everything come right. Now they saw that he meant only to use his powers to help those in trouble.

"He'll never be a King!" they said to one another. "He's a fraud! All he cares about is preaching and healing the sick. That's no use to us! We want someone who can deliver us from our hated enemies, the Romans, and win battles against them."

Many people, too, were annoyed because Jesus spoke well of

despised folk such as the Samaritans. "He even told a story the other day, in which the hero was a Samaritan!" said the people. "Everyone knows what the Samaritans are like. If Jesus thinks he is going to change our ideas about people like the Samaritans, he is wrong. We don't want to listen to things like that."

Caiaphas and the others had their spies going among the people of Jerusalem, and they rejoiced when news was brought that the people seemed to be turning against Jesus.

"There are still many for him," said the spies, "but there are now also many against him. The time will soon come when it will be safe to arrest him and bring him to be judged."

And so Caiaphas waited impatiently for word to come from Judas. The time was drawing near.

47: THE LAST SUPPER

Jesus very much wanted to eat the sacred Feast of the Passover with his disciples before he was betrayed by Judas. This feast was always held at the beginning of the Festival Week.

On the day of the feast the disciples came to Jesus and asked him where they should all eat the Passover Supper. Jesus did not tell them exactly where because he did not want Judas to know, in case he betrayed him too soon. So he spoke to Peter and John, giving them directions.

"Go to the city," Jesus said, "and at the gate you will meet a man carrying a pitcher of water on his head. Follow him to the house that he enters. Go inside and speak to the master of the house. Say to him, 'The Master says to you, where is the guest-room in which I may eat the Passover Feast with my disciples?'

"And the man will show you a large upper room, furnished ready. There you can prepare the feast for us."

So Peter and John went to the city where, at the gate, they met a man bearing a pitcher of water on his head. They followed him through the streets and saw him go into a house. They went there too, and spoke to the master of the house, saying exactly what Jesus had told them to say.

The man, who must have been a friend of Jesus, and who had probably promised to lend him a room when he needed it, at once took Peter and John upstairs and showed them a large room. There was a table for the feast, and drawn around the table were couches. In those days people ate their meals lying on couches, not sitting on chairs. Two or three people used a couch, and reclined on their left arms, eating with their right hands. The room was large enough to take Jesus and his twelve disciples; and Peter and John set about preparing the feast at once.

There had to be bread, made without yeast, a sauce made of different things, a bitter salad, roast lamb, and wine to drink. It was easy to get all these things in Festival Week in Jerusalem, and by the time that Jesus and his disciples arrived at the house, everything was ready.

The disciples went to their places round the table, and some of them wanted to take the chief seats. Jesus noticed this and he was sad. Had they understood so little of his preaching that they did not yet understand such things did not matter? It was not where a man sat that mattered, nor what honour was paid him – it was the good or bad in his heart that were the important things.

Jesus had come to help and to serve others, and his disciples knew it. They called him Master, but he was their willing and loving servant, as they very well knew, and the servant of anyone in trouble.

Now there was no servant there that night to welcome them, and to bring water to wash their dusty feet, as the custom was in that country. So Jesus himself decided to be the servant, and to show his disciples that, although he was their leader and master, he was pleased to be their servant, too.

He arose from his couch and took off his long cloak and wide belt. He tied a big towel round his waist just as servants did. Then he poured water into a basin and set it on the floor. The disciples looked on in wonder. But when they saw Jesus was about to wash their feet, they were ashamed, especially those who had quarrelled about the chief places at the feast.

Jesus went from one man to another, washing their dusty feet, and wiping them dry with the towel he had tied round his waist. When he came to Peter, Peter tried to stop him from washing his feet, but Jesus went on with his loving work. Then the disciples knew very plainly what Jesus meant when he said to them, "He that would be chiefest among you shall be servant of all."

Then the Feast began. Jesus took the bread, blessed it and broke it, giving it to each of his disciples. He gave them the cup of wine, telling them all to drink of it. Then he told them that the broken bread and the red wine were like his body, which should be broken, and his blood, which should be poured out. He was giving them his body and his blood.

Soon he was to die. He was to die because he had dared to

preach a kingdom of love, because he had dared to try and turn people from wrongdoing to good. But, Jesus told his disciples, he was glad to die for such a cause, for then and ever after people would know that he loved them and had come to save them from their sins. But after he was dead, he told them, he would rise again in three days' time.

The disciples shared the bread and the wine with him, and Jesus told them that after his death he would again share the same things with them. Then, when he had gone away never to return to them, they should keep the sharing of the bread and wine in remembrance of him.

And to this day we keep this simple feast, which we call the Holy Communion. When we keep it, we remember how he gave his body and his blood for all those who welcome his kingdom of love, and how he died because he dared to try and save the world from evil.

The disciples were sad when Jesus spoke of dying, and of leaving them. Peter spoke up bravely:

"Lord!" he said. "I am ready to go with you, both into prison and to death."

Then Jesus looked sadly at Peter, and said: "I tell you, Peter, before the cock crows twice, this very night you will deny three times that you know me!"

"No, no," said Peter, and he meant it with all his heart. "I will never deny you, never desert you, Master!" And the rest of the disciples said the same. But Jesus would not alter what he had said.

Then he said something that astonished the little company very much. "One of you here, sitting at table with me, will betray me to my enemies," said Jesus, with such sadness in his voice that all the disciples looked at him, grieving.

Then they looked at one another, wondering whom Jesus meant. A traitor among them? But surely each men there loved Jesus with all his heart. They began to ask him who the traitor was, saying, "Master, is it I? Master, you surely don't mean *me*?"

Now, next to Jesus, on his couch, was a disciple whom Jesus loved very much. This was John. Peter signed to him to ask Jesus who the traitor was. So John leaned back towards his Master and asked him the question that was in everyone's heart:

"Lord, who is the traitor?"

And Jesus answered John, saying, "The one to whom I shall give a sop of bread dipped in the sauce is the one who will betray me."

Judas said in a low voice, "Master, is it I?"

Then Jesus took a sop of bread, dipped it in the sauce, and gave it to Judas. And Judas said, in a low voice, "Master, is it I?"

And Jesus said, "Yes, it is you. Go, Judas, and do what you have to do quickly."

Then Judas got up from his couch at once. He knew that Jesus had guessed his fearful secret. He went quickly out of the room into the darkness of night.

No one knew why Jesus had sent Judas away. They thought he had gone to buy something for the feast out of the money he kept in the purse; or perhaps Jesus had sent him to give something to the poor. Only Judas knew why he had been sent. Jesus could no longer bear to have a traitor in that happy little company.

And then Jesus gave them a new commandment, the greatest of all. He gave it not only to his disciples, but to everyone.

"I give you a new commandment," he said. "Love one another. Even as I have loved you, love one another. Everyone shall know my friends and followers because they shall love one another."

Then Jesus rose, for it was time to be going. Out into the night he took his disciples, through the streets of Jerusalem to a quiet place he knew called the Garden of Gethsemane. He needed to be alone for a little while, and to pray.

48: IN THE GARDEN OF GETHSEMANE

When the disciples came to the gate of the garden, Jesus told them all to stay there, except for Peter, James and John. These three he wanted near him, for he was very unhappy.

He went into the dark and quiet garden with the three he had chosen. The olive trees spread their branches out over his head. Jesus was very miserable and sad, for he knew that his work was finished, that Judas was even now betraying him, and that in a short while terrible things would happen.

"My heart is full of sorrow," Jesus said to the three disciples, "sorrow as heavy as death. Will you wait for me here and keep awake?"

He left the three disciples and went a little way away. Then he fell on his knees and prayed.

Although Jesus was the Son of God, he was a man, with a man's body able to feel pain, and a man's heart able to suffer deep unhappiness. In this dark hour Jesus knew what terrible pain would come to him, and what depths of sorrow. He prayed to God that, if it were possible, God should save him from the terrible things that were coming to him.

"Yet not my will, but your will must be done," he prayed. He needed all the courage that any man would need, and more, because he was not only the Son of Man, but the Son of God too.

Then, feeling lonely and sad, he went back to feel the warmth of a few words with the three disciples who loved him greatly. But they were all asleep.

Then he said to them, sadly: "Could you not keep awake for me one hour?"

Then Jesus went away again, and prayed once more. It was so hard for him to accept God's will that night – he could have escaped, perhaps; he could even have used his miraculous powers to defend himself from his enemies. And yet he knew that it was not what he himself wanted, that he must choose, but what God had willed. It was a hard, sorrowful, lonely way that the spirit of Jesus had to travel that night.

He went back a second time to his disciples, and again they were all asleep. Their hearts were heavy, and they could not keep their eyes open. Jesus looked at them, sad and lonely, but said nothing. He went away by himself for the third time, and again prayed to God, his Father, for help to bear his agony.

But when Jesus went once more back to his three disciples, his face was no longer full of misery, but shone with high courage.

"Rise," he said. "Let us be going. The one who has betrayed me is here."

Jesus was right. Judas had been to the High Priest, and had told him that he would find Jesus that night in the Garden of Gethsamane, alone with his disciples. It would be easy to arrest him there.

49: JESUS IS CAPTURED

Even as Jesus warned his disciples that the time of betrayal was near, there came the noise of men walking in at the garden gate, the sound of voices, and the light of lanterns and torches flaring in the night.

Judas was at the head of the crowd. There were the servants of the High Priest, the Temple Guard, some of the chief priests and elders, and a company of soldiers, too. They were all armed with swords or sticks, and the light of their many torches sent strange shadows racing here and there in the Garden of Gethsemane.

"How shall we know which man is Jesus?" his enemies asked Judas.

"I will go and kiss the man you want," said Judas. "Watch to see whom it is I greet, and then take him."

So Judas went up to Jesus, who was waiting quietly beneath the olive-trees, and kissed him. "Hail, Master!" he said, as he had said so often before.

"Judas!" said Jesus, sternly and sadly. "Do you betray me with a kiss?"

Then Jesus went to meet the crowd of men at the gate, and said, "Whom do you seek?"

And they said, "Jesus of Nazareth."

"I am he," said Jesus. But the crowd of men did not press forward to arrest him at once. There was something about Jesus that made them shrink back, half-afraid.

Then Jesus said to them again, "Whom do you seek?"

And again they said, "Jesus of Nazareth."

"I have told you that I am Jesus of Nazareth," said Jesus. "If you have come only to find me, then let these friends of mine go."

But Peter drew a sword and began to strike at the nearest man. "Put up your sword," said Jesus to Peter. Then he turned to the crowd.

"Do you come to take me with swords and staves as if I were a thief or a robber? Did I not sit in the Temple each day, preaching, and you laid no hand on me? But now your time has come and the dark powers must have their way."

Then all his disciples forsook him and fled, even Peter. Jesus was alone with his enemies.

50: BEFORE THE COCK CREW TWICE

It was not long before Jesus was seized and his hands tied tightly. Then out of the quiet garden he was taken, the crowd shouting behind him, their lanterns and torches shining in the night.

He was taken to the palace of the High Priest to be questioned and accused. The house of Caiaphas, a very grand mansion indeed, was built all round a big central courtyard. Jesus was taken in through the great gate, and when everyone was in the courtyard, or in the house itself, the gate was shut.

Now Peter longed to know what was happening to Jesus. He had run away with the other disciples, but after a while he followed the crowd, and came to the palace of Caiaphas. He longed to be with Jesus and yet he was afraid.

He managed to get through the gate and into the big courtyard. It was full of servants and soldiers. As the night was cold, one of the servants had lighted a big fire in the middle of the courtyard, and Peter, feeling cold and miserable, went to the glowing flames to warm himself.

A little crowd of men and women were also sitting near the fire, warming themselves. Peter sat down among them. Then a maid-servant, seeing his face in the light of the fire, looked closely at him. "Now where have I seen this man before?" she thought. Then she knew, and she exclaimed out loud, turning to Peter.

"You are one of the disciples of that man Jesus, aren't you?"

But Peter was afraid and answered at once. "Woman, I don't know Jesus at all!"

And in the distance a cock crew loudly, for daybreak was not far off.

Presently someone else saw Peter, and felt sure he was a disciple. "You are one of them!" he said to Peter.

But Peter shook his head and answered loudly, "Man, I am not!"

And after a time, hearing Peter speak, someone said, "I am quite sure this man is one of Jesus' friends, because you can tell by his speech that he comes from Galilee."

Then Peter, full of fear, began to curse and to swear. "I tell you I don't even *know* this Jesus you talk of!" he vowed.

And then the cock crew for the second time, for it was dawn. Jesus was then in the courtyard, and he heard Peter shouting that he did not know him. He turned and looked at his disciple with such sadness in his eyes that Peter's heart almost broke.

He remembered what Jesus had said – that before the cock crew twice, he would deny his master three times – and he had done so, although he had vowed that he never would. He had vowed that he would go to prison, and even be put to death for Jesus' sake – and yet, so short a time after, he had been too afraid even to say that he knew Jesus.

Then Peter went out into the street and wept bitterly.

51: THE TRIAL OF JESUS

Now Caiaphas and the rulers of the Jews had to find some good reason to condemn Jesus to punishment. So they set to work to find people who would tell them things against Jesus. What had he done wrong? Let them hear of just one thing, and they would accuse Jesus of it and condemn him.

But Jesus had never done wrong. He had kept all the laws. He had never done anything but good. It was difficult to find anything against him at all.

There were plenty of people who made up all kinds of things that Jesus had said, and they hastened to tell their lies to the council that Caiaphas had called. But none of the lies seemed to agree, and the council grew confused.

Then Caiaphas stood up and spoke sternly to Jesus, who stood with his hands tied, saying and answering nothing.

"I ask you to tell me if you are the Christ, the Son of the Blessed One?" said Caiaphas.

And Jesus answered at once, "I am! And in time to come you shall see the Son of Man sitting on the right hand of God's power, and coming in the clouds of Heaven!"

Then Caiaphas fell into a rage and tore his clothes, and cried, "He has blasphemed! He has spoken terrible things of God! What need have we of any further witnesses? We have all heard this blasphemy – he has called himself the Christ!"

Jesus *was* the Saviour, the Christ, and he was not speaking blasphemy but the truth. But nobody believed him. Caiaphas was full of triumph. At last they could accuse Jesus and condemn him.

"What do you think now?" cried Caiaphas to the council. And they all cried but one thing.

"Put him to death!"

And then Jesus had to suffer mockery and pain from those about him. They spat in his face, and struck him. They put a cloth over his eyes, and then hit him with the palms of their hands, crying. "You say you are the Christ; well, tell us who is striking you now! You say you are the Son of the Blessed One – surely you can tell who is striking you."

And so, tired and lonely and sad, mocked at and struck, Jesus passed that night alone among his enemies, wondering what the coming day would bring to him.

52: JESUS GOES BEFORE PILATE, THE ROMAN GOVERNOR

The Jews themselves had no power to put anyone to death. They had to get Pilate, the Roman Governor of Judaea, to give them permission to do that. So they dragged Jesus off, early in the morning, to the beautiful castle where Pilate lived.

Pilate was a cruel man, who hated the Jews. He was also rather afraid of them, for he knew that if he did too many cruel things, they might send a complaint about him to the Roman Emperor.

He received the message, early that morning, that the Jews were bringing to him a dangerous prisoner. So, when Jesus was brought into his big courtyard, Pilate was ready to judge the case. He appeared on the balcony overlooking the courtyard, and saw Jesus standing there, a prisoner, with his hands tied.

"What charge do you bring against him?" asked Pilate.

The Jews hardly knew what to say. Pilate would only laugh if they said that they had condemned Jesus because he had called himself the Son of God.

So they answered and said that the charge against him didn't matter. They themselves had found Jesus guilty and had condemned him to death. It was now for Pilate to carry out the sentence, for they, the Jews, had no power to do so.

"Well, deal with the matter yourselves," said Pilate, who did not like the surly tone of the Jews. He felt sure, too, that they had not any real grievance against Jesus, for Pilate had heard something about him, and guessed that the Chief Priests and Elders were jealous of his hold over the people.

"But we have no power to put anyone to death!" said the Jews, in dismay; and they began to whisper together to see if they could think of something which would make the Roman Governor do what they wanted him to do.

"It's no good saying that Jesus says he is the Christ," said one. "Pilate would laugh at us. The Romans always scoff at our religion. We must think of something else."

"Has Jesus ever said or done anything against the Romans?" said another. "Pilate would have to take notice if we could bring a charge of that sort against him."

"We'll say that Jesus has been telling the people wrong things," said a third. "We'll say that he told them not to pay their taxes to the Roman Emperor, because he himself is their King! Doesn't he keep talking about his kingdom? Well, surely the Romans would be against a man who sets himself up to be king of a country which *they* rule!"

"That is a very good idea," said the others. "Pilate wouldn't bother about our Jewish rules being broken – but he will *have* to take notice if we say that our charges all have to do with the Roman Government!"

So they told Pilate these things, and the whole court heard them. Jesus heard them too, but he said nothing, even when Pilate gave him a chance to speak.

Then the Roman Governor decided to take Jesus alone with him into the castle, and ask him questions. It was difficult to find out anything when the Jews kept shouting, and the prisoner kept silent.

Pilate soon decided that Jesus should not be put to death. It was clear that this man was not the kind to lead an army against the Romans! Pilate would tell the Jews his decision.

So he went out on his balcony once more and sat on his judgment seat. He spoke loudly to the chief priests and the people in the courtyard.

"I find no fault in this man," said Pilate, who meant to set Jesus free, when he had told the people this.

When the crowd heard these words, they were very angry. They began to shout and yell at the tops of their voices.

"He *is* guilty!"

"He's always stirring up the people!"

"He tries to turn the Jews against the Roman Government!"

"He's been all over Judaea teaching these things! He started in Galilee, and stirred up the people from there to here!"

Pilate listened to the shouts. He suddenly heard the word "Galilee", and an idea came to him.

Herod ruled over Galilee, not Pilate. If this man came from Galilee, then Herod should judge his case, not Pilate. Herod was in Jerusalem that very day. It would be a good idea to send Jesus to Herod to be judged, and then, he, Pilate, need have nothing more to do with the man.

So Jesus was dragged off to Herod's palace in Jerusalem. He was tired and unhappy and lonely. With his hands still tied he was taken before Herod.

Now Herod had heard all about Jesus and the wonders he had done. He was very pleased to see him.

"Perhaps he will do a miracle for me to see!" thought Herod. So he began to question Jesus eagerly.

Jesus before Pilate

"Surely, in order to be set free, he will be willing to do a fine miracle for me!" thought Herod. But to his surprise, Jesus said nothing. What use was there in saying anything?

All the time the chief priests and the rulers were standing by, shouting spitefully about Jesus. It was a horrible scene. In the end Herod lost his temper and began to mock at Jesus too.

"So you're a king, are you!" he said. "Well, we'll dress you up as one! Fetch one of my cloaks, and we will drape it round the great king who stands so silent before us!"

So a gorgeous cloak was fetched and put on Jesus. Then Herod and his soldiers made fun of him and mocked him cruelly. When they had finished, Herod sent him back to Pilate, still wearing the gorgeous cloak, so that everyone might laugh at him.

When Pilate heard that Herod had sent Jesus back to him, he decided to tell the people that he would not put Jesus to death. So he spoke to them.

"You brought this man before me on a charge of stirring up the people," he said. "I have examined him before you, and I find nothing against him. Neither does Herod find any fault in him worthy of death. I will therefore have him beaten and then set him free."

Now at the Festival of the Passover it was the custom that the Roman Governor should set free any prisoner whom the people begged for. Pilate thought that he would set Jesus free, for he knew that the Jews would expect him to keep up the old custom.

But the Jews were not going to have Jesus set free! No – they would rather have any prisoner freed than Jesus!

"Away with this man!" they cried. "We don't want him to be set free. Give us Barabbas instead!"

Now Barabbas was a well-known robber and murderer, and it was astonishing that the Jews would sooner have one who robbed and killed them, than Jesus, who had never done anything but good. But now the crowd was beside itself with anger, because Pilate would not condemn Jesus to death, and even suggested setting him free.

Now just at this moment a servant came up to Pilate with a message from his wife. She was a good woman, whose words were worth listening to.

Pilate read the message. "Do nothing with this good man," his wife had written. "I have dreamt about him to-day, and the dream frightened me very much."

All this time the chief priests were going about the crowd of people, telling them that they must go on shouting for Barabbas to be set free, and ask for Jesus to be killed. They worked the mob into a fury, so that when Pilate asked them again they should shout all the more loudly for Barabbas.

"Now which prisoner shall I set free?" said Pilate. "Barabbas – or Jesus?"

"Barabbas, Barabbas, Barabbas!" shouted the mob.

"Then what shall I do with Jesus?" asked Pilate, wondering if the people might ask for his release, as well as for the other prisoner's.

The people made a terrible answer. "Let him be crucified!"

"But what evil has he done?" cried Pilate, amazed and dismayed at the violence of the Jews.

"Crucify him!" shouted the crowd. "Take him to the cross! Crucify him!"

And then Pilate saw that he could do nothing more. Barabbas the robber and murderer must be set free, and Jesus must be killed. But Pilate was not comfortable in his mind about the matter, for he felt sure that Jesus was not worthy of death.

He sent a servant for a basin of water, and, before all the people, he washed his hands.

"I am washing my hands to show you that I wish to be clean in this matter!" he told the people. "I am innocent of the blood of this good man. I am not to blame for his death. It is your choice, not mine!"

And all the Jews cried out with one voice. "We will take the blame! His blood be on us and on our children!"

53: JESUS IS PUNISHED

Pilate set Barabbas free, and the robber went gladly out of prison, free to rob and kill again if he wished.

But Jesus was taken to be cruelly beaten. The soldiers carried out the punishment, and then dragged Jesus into their barracks to make fun of him. They had no pity for a bleeding man, no mercy for someone tired, in pain and unhappy.

No – here was someone delivered into their hands, someone completely at their mercy. They would taunt him and mock him, before they put him to death!

"This fellow has called himself King of the Jews!" said one soldier. "Let's crown him and give him a sceptre, and pretend to bow down to him."

So the soldiers stripped the clothes from Jesus, and found a scarlet robe for him. They gave him a chair to sit on for a throne.

"And now what shall we give him for a crown?" said a soldier, laughing. "And he must have a sceptre, too!"

Now in those days kings often wore wreaths made of leaves for crowns. It was easy to make a crown of that sort for Jesus – but why not make the wreath of something thorny, so that it would hurt?

Before long a soldier had plaited a crown of thorns, and set it roughly on Jesus' head. Then a stick was put into his hand for a sceptre.

All the soldiers stood round, laughing and mocking. "Now let's do homage to the king!" they cried. "We will each go up and bow low."

And then one by one the soldiers went up to Jesus, and bowed low in mockery, crying, "Hail, King of the Jews!"

When they had bowed, they stood upright and spat in his face. Some of them took the stick they had given him for a sceptre and hit him about the face with it. To the soldiers it was great sport to taunt a defenceless man.

The soldiers took Jesus to Pilate dressed up in the red cloak, and with the crown of thorns on his head. It was a pitiful sight.

Pilate spoke to the people. "Behold, I bring this man Jesus to you, so that you may know I find no fault in him." Perhaps Pilate thought that if the people saw Jesus so tormented and hurt they would no longer cry out for his death.

"Now look at him!" said Pilate. But the Jews had no pity in their hearts at all for Jesus. They could only shout one thing:

"Crucify him, crucify him!"

Then, because some of them felt that Pilate was still doing all he could to set Jesus free, they thought of something else to shout.

"You are no friend of the Emperor's if you let this man go! Doesn't he say he is a king? What would your Emperor, Cæsar, say, if he heard that? You are no friend of Cæsar's."

Then Pilate was afraid, and handed Jesus over to the chief priests to be killed. And they took Jesus and led him away.

54: WHAT HAPPENED TO THE TRAITOR

Now what was the traitor Judas doing all this time? Was he rejoicing in his betrayal of Jesus, glad to think that his Master was suffering so much?

Judas had begun to feel sorry for what he had done. He knew that Jesus had been found guilty, and he had heard that he was to be taken before Pilate, so that the Roman Governor might order him to be put to death.

Then into the heart of Judas there came many memories – thoughts of the kind deeds Jesus had done, the good words he had said, the mercy he had shown to everyone. Judas knew that Jesus was innocent. Because his disciple had betrayed him, Jesus, the noblest man that Judas had ever known, was going to be cruelly put to death.

Judas hated himself, He repented bitterly. He could not think how he could have done such a thing. Jesus had loved him, and Judas had repaid him by betrayal and death.

Judas looked at the thirty pieces of silver that had seemed to him to be such a good reward for a few words of betrayal. They seemed terrible to him now. He could never spend them. They were the price of innocent blood. But what was he to do?

He could not save Jesus; he knew that. Things had gone too far. The man was in despair. He was so ashamed and so unhappy that he had to do something to try and ease his mind.

"I will go and give the money back to the chief priests who gave it to me!" he thought, suddenly. "I can at least do that. Not all of them will be in Pilate's courtyard. Some of them will be in the Temple, preparing the Passover Festival. I will go there."

So, wild and haggard with terrible remorse and shame, Judas set off to the Temple. The chief priests there were astonished to see him.

"I have sinned," said Judas, his misery showing in his unhappy face. "I have done a terrible wrong. I have betrayed an innocent man."

"You should have thought of that before," said the priests. "What do *we* care? It has nothing to do with us!"

"Here's your money back!" cried Judas, and he flung the thirty pieces of silver down on the floor of the Temple. They rolled about everywhere.

And then Judas the traitor, knowing that he could never be happy again, went out of the Temple and hanged himself.

It would have been better if he had gone to Jesus, for he would have been forgiven, and might have lived to do good work for the Master he had betrayed.

55: JESUS IS CRUCIFIED

There were two other prisoners in the jail, who were to be put to death that day with Jesus. They were robbers who had belonged to the band of Barabbas. Pilate gave orders that they were to go to the cross with Jesus.

Each prisoner had to carry the heavy cross-piece over his shoulders on his way to be crucified. A cross was in two parts – the upright piece, which was driven into the ground – and the cross-piece, which the prisoners had to carry.

Around their necks the prisoners had to wear a placard, saying who they were and what their crime was. Pilate had made out the placard for Jesus. He had written "THE KING OF THE JEWS". Pilate knew that this would make the chief priests angry, and it certainly did. But Pilate would not alter what he had written.

The soldiers took away the red cloak they had dressed Jesus in, when they wanted to make fun of him, and gave him back his own clothes. Then they laid the heavy cross-piece over his shoulders, and did the same to the two robbers.

It was a long way to the hill where the crosses were set up. Jesus was tired and weak. He had had no sleep, he had been cruelly beaten, and he had been dragged from place to place for hours. And now the passers-by began to follow the three bearing their crosses, and to shout and mock at them.

"Ho, look at this one!" someone cried. "See what is written on his placard: 'THE KING OF THE JEWS'! How comical! He doesn't look like a king, does he?"

Jesus carried the heavy cross-piece, but he was so weak that he began to stumble under the great weight. The soldiers kicked him up when he fell, but soon he fell so often that it was clear the little procession would take a long time to get to the place where the crosses were. So the soldiers looked around for someone to bear the cross-piece for Jesus.

They reached out into the crowd and took hold of a man there called Simon of Cyrene. "Carry this man's cross for him,"

Jesus carrying the cross . . .

they commanded. And Simon was forced to carry the cross for Jesus. Then Jesus was able to walk more easily.

Whilst some people jeered and mocked, there were women who wept and wailed. Some of them had heard Jesus talking in the Temple, and had seen him heal the sick. Jesus turned and spoke to them.

"Do not weep for me," he said sadly. "Weep for yourselves and your children, for there are terrible days coming!"

Jesus was taken out of the city to a hill called Golgotha. There the soldiers nailed his hands and feet to the big wooden cross, and he hung there with a crucified robber on each side of him.

The robbers cursed and swore with the terrible pain, but Jesus bore it with courage.

"Father, forgive them, for they know not what they do," he said.

Then, whilst the three hung there in the hot sun, suffering great pain and shame, people came to look at them and to jeer. They read what was written on the boards above the heads of the three crucified men. When they saw what was written on the board at the top of Jesus' cross, they laughed loudly.

"JESUS OF NAZARETH, KING OF THE JEWS" was written on the board. It was written in three languages, so that no matter what part of the country the people passing by came from, they could all read it.

The enemies of Jesus came to taunt him as he hung on the cross. "Ho! Didn't you save others? Well, why don't you save yourself now? You are not so clever as you thought you were!"

"He says he is the Son of God!" said others. "Well, why doesn't he show his power and come down from the cross?"

And even the watching soldiers mocked him and shouted, "Aren't you the King of the Jews? Well, set yourself free, then!"

Then the two robbers on the crosses beside him began to jeer at him too. Jesus answered nothing, but hung there patiently in great pain.

"If you're the Saviour, why don't you save yourself and us too?" cried one robber. The other turned his head and looked at Jesus. What he saw in that patient, kindly face made him feel ashamed. He began to rebuke the other robber.

"You and I have done wrong, and we are being punished for it," he said. "But this man has done no wrong." Then he turned to Jesus.

"Lord," he said, "remember me when you come into your kingdom."

Jesus answered him gladly, "To-day you shall be with me in Paradise."

Not far from the crosses a few friends of Jesus stood, grieving bitterly for him. They knew he was in terrible pain; they knew he was dying, and they could do nothing for him at all.

John was there, the disciple whom Jesus loved most, and with him stood Mary, the mother of Jesus, bewildered and unhappy to see her noble son hanging on the cross between two robbers. Jesus saw them both, and saw how his mother grieved. Who would love her and look after her now that he was dying?

He saw John comforting her, as if he were her own son. Then Jesus spoke to them both.

"Behold your son!" he said to his mother. And to John he said, "Behold your mother!"

And both knew what he meant. John was to look after Mary as if she were his own mother, and she was to turn to John as if he were her son. So, from that day, John took Mary into his own home, and cared for her like a son.

Even in his agony Jesus could think of those he loved – and it was indeed agony now. Jesus had to bear it all, because he had made up his mind that it was the only way to show men that he really loved them. But he was in such pain and so weak that his spirit was weighed down with dark unhappiness. He felt that he was terribly alone, and in the darkest hour of his life he cried out the words of a psalm he had learnt as a boy.

"My God, my God, why have you forsaken me?"

The sun beat down, and Jesus was thirsty. One of the soldiers heard his voice, weak and faint: "I thirst."

The man ran to a bowl of sour wine standing nearby, and dipped a sponge into it. It soaked up the liquid. Then the soldier set the sponge on the end of a stick and held it up to Jesus. Jesus was able to take a little of the liquid to quench his terrible thirst. The small kindness must have touched him in his dark hour.

Then Jesus said, "It is finished!" He was about to die, and he knew it. His life of love and kindness was ending.

He gave a loud cry. "Father, into your hands I entrust my spirit!" His weary head drooped, and he became still. Jesus of Nazareth was dead.

The captain of the soldiers had sat near the crosses since the three men had been hung there. He had heard all that Jesus had said. He had noticed his kindness to his mother, and to one of the robbers. He had heard the loud cry, almost of triumph, when Jesus had died.

"Truly this was a good man!" said the captain. "He must have been the Son of God!"

Then came a man called Joseph of Arimathæa. He had been a secret follower of Jesus, and he had loved him. He had not dared to proclaim his faith in Jesus when he was alive, but he felt that he must do something for him in death.

So he went to Pilate and asked him if he might have the body of Jesus to bury. Pilate gave him permission, and Joseph and some other friends took the still body down from the cross, pulled out the cruel nails, and wrapped Jesus in sweet-smelling linen, into which they put fragrant spices.

Joseph had a tomb in a garden not far from where the crosses had been put up. It was a cool cave in which no one had ever been buried before. Joseph took the body of Jesus there, and then sadly left the tomb, rolling across the entrance a heavy stone to block the doorway.

A few women, who had been near the cross, grieving and weeping, watched the men rolling the stone in front of the cave. "We will come here again as soon as we can," the women said to one another. "There is not much we can do for Jesus now, but we will bring sweet spices to the cave, and anoint him."

56: JESUS COMES AGAIN

The disciples of Jesus were full of terror and despair when they knew all that had happened to their beloved Master. They could not believe it! It had all happened so suddenly. This wonderful man, their constant friend and companion, who had done so many miracles, and who had always been so strong and wise, had been hung upon a cross between two robbers, and had died there!

The disciples hid themselves away in Jerusalem, fearing that they might be captured and put to death too. They forgot that Jesus had said he would rise again in three days' time. They felt sure they would never see him again.

They were utterly dismayed. Whilst the sounds of gladness were going on in the city, where the people were keeping the great Festival, the disciples grieved bitterly. It seemed to them as if their whole world had fallen to pieces.

Now, very early in the morning of the third day, some of the women who had loved Jesus set out to go to his tomb, with the sweet spices they had bought. They talked sadly together as they went.

"I know exactly where the cave is," said one. "I saw where his body was laid, and I was there when the tomb was closed by rolling a big stone across it."

"A big stone!" said another woman. "Was it very heavy? Can we move it?"

The women were dismayed when they thought of the heavy stone across the entrance of the cave.

"Who will move it for us?" they wondered.

As the sun was rising, the women came to the garden of the tomb. Then they had a great surprise. Not far off was the tomb – but there was no stone in front of it! Someone had moved it away.

The women stood in astonishment. They went forward to the tomb and entered the cave. The body of Jesus was no longer there – but, sitting on the right side of the tomb they saw what they thought to be a young man, dressed in a long and dazzling white robe.

The women were terrified. What could have happened? Where was the body of Jesus? Who was this strangely beautiful young man?

He spoke to them kindly, for he saw their great fear. "Don't be afraid! You are looking for Jesus of Nazareth, who was crucified. He is risen. He is not here. Look! Here is the place where his body was laid."

The women listened, amazed and afraid. Could this being be an angel?

"Go on your way," said the young man. "Tell Jesus' disciples, especially Peter, that he will go before them to Galilee, and that they will see him there, as he told them."

The women were trembling with amazement and fear. They did not know what to think. Had Jesus really gone? Had he come to life again? Who was this strange being in the tomb, who spoke to them so kindly, and told them to take a message from Jesus to his disciples?

They turned and fled out of the cave into the early morning sunshine. They ran back all the way they had come, their hearts full of wonder and fear. Jesus had risen from the dead! What would the disciples say to their amazing news?

The disciples listened in astonishment. They could not believe it was true. Peter and John sprang up at once, and ran as fast as they could to the garden of the tomb, to see for themselves if what the women had said was true. Their words echoed in their ears as they ran. "They have taken away the Master out of the tomb, and we do not know where they have laid him."

The two men ran fast, but John, who was the younger of the two, got to the tomb first. He stooped down and looked inside, wondering what he would see. There was no body there – only the white linen grave-clothes lying on one side of the cave.

As John stood there, hardly knowing whether to go in or not, Peter came up, panting. He went into the tomb at once. There he saw the grave-clothes lying, but Jesus was not there. Peter was amazed. What the women had said was true! It was glorious news.

Then John went into the tomb, and he too saw with certainty that Jesus was not there. "We must go back and tell the others," said Peter. "Now we know what our Master meant when he said that he would rise again in three days' time. This is the third day."

The disciples left the empty tomb and went back to tell the others what they had seen. If only they could see Jesus! That would really prove to them that he had come to life again.

One of the women who loved Jesus, called Mary Magdalene, also went to the garden that morning, and came weeping to the tomb where she had seen Joseph put the poor, still body of Jesus. She too saw that the stone had been rolled away from the cave, and she stooped down and looked into the tomb.

To her great amazement she saw two angels sitting there, one where the head of Jesus had lain, and the other where his feet had been. As she looked at them in the utmost surprise, they spoke to her.

"Why do you weep?" they asked.

"Because they have taken away the body of my Lord, and I do not know where they have laid him," said Mary Magdalene, sorrowfully.

Then she felt that someone else was near her, and she turned round to see who it was, though she was blinded by her tears. She saw someone she thought was the gardener.

"Why do you weep?" he said, tenderly. "Whom are you looking for?"

"Oh sir!" cried Mary, the tears running down her cheeks. "If you have taken him somewhere, tell me where you have laid him, and I will take him away!"

And then the man whom Mary had mistaken for the gardener said one word to her, so tenderly and lovingly that she knew who he was.

"Mary!" he said.

She turned to him and cried out gladly. "My Master!" She knew it was the voice of Jesus, whom she loved so much. She fell on her knees to worship him, and a great gladness filled her heart.

57: JESUS COMES TO HIS DISCIPLES

On the evening of that day, two disciples of Jesus set out to walk from Jerusalem to the village of Emmaus, their home. They talked as they went, and their talk, of course, was all of the happenings of the last few days.

They spoke of their Master, Jesus, and of the terrible things that had happened to him. They were sad, and, although they had heard something of what had happened in the garden of the tomb, they found it difficult to believe.

Now, as they walked, someone caught up with them and walked beside them. Darkness was coming on, and the disciples could not see very clearly.

It was Jesus who was beside them, Jesus who walked with them in the twilight on the road to Emmaus. He spoke to them.

"What is it you are saying to one another that makes you look so sad?"

"You must surely be a stranger in Jerusalem if you do not know the terrible things that have happened there in the last few days!" said Cleopas, one of the disciples.

"What things?" asked the stranger.

"About Jesus of Nazareth," said Cleopas. "He was a wonderful man, mighty in deed and word before God and all the people. He was condemned by the priests and the rulers, and they crucified him."

"You see," said the other disciple, "we hoped and believed he might save Israel and its people. Now we have no hope left."

"One strange thing has happened," said Cleopas: "Some women who went to his tomb this morning found it empty and they came back to us, saying they had seen angels who told them Jesus was alive. Some of our friends went to see if what the women said was true – but they didn't see Jesus."

Then the stranger began to speak to them wisely. "Oh, foolish ones, how slow you are to believe all that the prophets have spoken! Do you not see that the Saviour had to suffer all these things before he entered into his glory?"

And then the stranger talked to them of all the wise sayings written in their Bibles, things that had been written years and years before by wise men who foretold the coming of Jesus, and who set down the things that were to happen when he came. The disciples listened in amazement, and began to understand many things they had never understood before. They began to see why Jesus had had to suffer, and why, although he could help others, he would not use his power to help himself.

Soon they were at the village of Emmaus, and the stranger made as though he was going on further. But the disciples could not part with this wonderful new friend.

"Stay with us!" they begged. "It is almost night and the day is far gone!"

So he went into their house with them, and sat down to a meal. And then, as Jesus had so often done before, he took bread, blessed it and broke it, giving some to each of them.

Then the two disciples knew that the wise stranger was Jesus himself, their beloved Master. They looked at him with wide eyes – and even as they looked, he vanished out of their sight.

"It was Jesus!" said Cleopas, his heart full of joy. "We might have known it. Didn't our hearts burn within us when he talked to us on the way, explaining so many things to us?"

"We must go straight back to Jerusalem and tell the others!" said his companion. So, though the night was come and it was late, the two set off joyfully on the long road back to Jerusalem.

When they got there they found a big company of the disciples gathered together, and they told them all that had happened.

"We didn't know it was Jesus until he took the bread, blessed it and broke it as he so often did!" said Cleopas. "Then our eyes were opened and we knew him!"

Now, even as the disciples spoke together of the strange and wonderful things that had happened that day, they saw that someone else was in the room with them. He had suddenly come, though how they did not know. He spoke to them in a voice they knew and loved.

"Peace to you all!"

The disciples were terrified. They gazed in fear at this man who had so suddenly and silently appeared in their midst. Could it be Jesus? They could not believe it. And yet it was his voice.

Jesus saw that they could not believe he really was there with them. "Why are you afraid?" he asked. "Why do you doubt that I am really here? Look at my hands and my feet – can't you see that it is really I myself? Feel me and see. A spirit has not got flesh and bones as I have!"

Then he held out to them his hands and showed them his feet, and they saw the wounds that the nails had made. They knew then without any doubt that it was Jesus himself, their beloved Master, and they cried out for joy.

One disciple, Thomas, was not with the others when Jesus came among them in this way, and he could not believe the news when the others told him.

"Jesus is dead and buried," said Thomas. "So many tales are going about now, relating strange things, but I find them difficult to believe. Now you say to me you have seen the Lord! Well, unless I see in his hands the marks of the nails, and put my fingers in his wounds, I will not believe it is Jesus."

In a week's time the disciples were once more gathered together, and the door was shut for fear of enemies. This time Thomas was with them.

And again Jesus came, and said, "Peace to you all!" And then he looked at Thomas, for he knew what Thomas had said.

"Take my hand and see the marks of the nails!" he said to Thomas. "Put your hand into my wounds! Do not doubt any more, but believe!"

But Thomas knew without any doubt that it was Jesus. "My Lord and my God!" he cried.

"Thomas," said Jesus, "because you have seen me you have believed; but blessed are those who do not see and yet believe!"

58: JESUS GOES TO GALILEE

Another time Jesus came to his disciples when they least expected it. They had gone back to Galilee, and Peter, tired of doing nothing, decided to take his boat and fish.

"I'm going fishing," he said to the others.

"We'll go too," they said, and they got into the boat and set out. All that night they fished and caught nothing.

When the morning came they looked towards the shore, and saw someone standing there. The stranger called to them.

"Have you anything to eat there?" he shouted.

"No!" they answered.

"Cast down your net on the right side of the boat, and you will catch plenty of fish," said the man on shore.

So they let down their net and it was at once so full of fish that they could not haul it up for the weight! This was very strange. John took a look at the stranger on the shore. He spoke to Peter eagerly.

"It is Jesus!"

When Peter heard this he sprang at once into the sea and swam to the shore. He had to get to Jesus! He could not wait one instant. The others came in a little boat from their ship, dragging the net full of fishes behind them.

When they got to the shore they saw that there was a fire burning, with fish cooking on it, and bread nearby.

"Bring some of the fish you have caught and we will have them too," said Jesus. So Peter went to get the net full of fish, and when they were counted, there were a hundred and fifty-three – and yet the net was not broken. John never forgot that, even when he was an old man.

"Come and eat," said Jesus. So they all ate their breakfast together, though not one of the disciples dared to ask if he really was their Lord come back again. But they soon found that Jesus was the same loving friend as ever.

Peter could not forget that three times he had denied that he knew Jesus, when his Master had been taken into the house of Caiaphas the High Priest. He could not help wondering if Jesus would trust him to work for him any more. Jesus knew this, and he took Peter aside and spoke to him gravely and lovingly.

"Simon," he said, calling Peter by the name he had before Jesus had given him the name of Peter, "Simon, do you love me more than these others?"

And Peter said, "Yes, Lord, you know I love you."

Then Jesus said, "Feed my lambs!" He meant that Peter was to help those who did not understand very much about God. Then he said to him again, "Simon, do you love me?"

And Peter answered for the second time, "Yes, Lord, you know I love you."

"Then feed my sheep," said Jesus, and this time he meant that Peter was to help those who knew more than the "lambs."

Again Jesus said to Peter, "Simon, do you love me?" Then Peter was grieved because Jesus asked him for the third time.

"You know everything, Lord," he said, "and so you must know that I love you."

"Then feed my sheep," said Jesus.

Three times Peter had denied his Lord, and now three times he had said that he loved him. Jesus trusted him again, and knew that he would be a strong rock on which to build his church. Peter was to feed his lambs and his sheep, he was to guide and help others. The disciple was very happy.

59: THE END OF THE STORY

For forty days Jesus remained on the earth, visiting his friends and disciples, cheering them and telling them what they must do. They must spread the good news to everyone, they must help the weak, they must teach the things that Jesus himself taught. They were the beginnings of his Church, they were the first Christians. There were to be many, many millions, all over the world, but to these few was given the honour of first spreading the good news.

And then there came a time when no one saw Jesus any more. The disciples said that he had ascended into heaven, in a cloud of glory, but they knew that he was with them always, in their hearts and minds, helping them and guiding them, just as he has helped and guided all those who have been his disciples and friends down the ages.

So ends the wonderful story of a wonderful man. Nearly two thousand years have passed since he was born, but the things he taught will never be forgotten.

And now I will end the story in the way I think Jesus would like me to end it – with the commandment he kept all the days of his life:

"LOVE ONE ANOTHER."